# MAKING SENSE OF COMPREHENSION

Mike Hamlin
David Jackson

Macmillan Education
London and Basingstoke

First published 1984

Published by
MACMILLAN EDUCATION LIMITED
Houndmills Basingstoke Hampshire RG21 2XS
and London
Associated companies throughout the world

Printed in Hong Kong


*British Library Cataloguing in Publication Data*

Hamlin, Michael
    Making sense of comprehension.
    1. English language
    I. Title        II. Jackson, David
    428.2        PE1128

    ISBN 0-333-36163-6

# CONTENTS

Introduction for teachers                                          1

**1** Asking your own questions                                   20
   'Uncle Albert' by Vernon Scannell
**2** Selecting key statements                                    23
   'The Library' from *Basketball Game* by Julius Lester
**3** Stepping into the writer's shoes                            28
   'First Day at School' by Roger McGough
**4** Giving shape to your thoughts I                             30
   'Prince Kano' by Edward Lowbury
**5** Key Questions I                                             34
   'The Place' by John Gordon
**6** Words into actions I                                        43
   'Poem for my Sister' by Liz Lochhead
**7** Filling in the gaps                                         46
   'The Secret in the Cat' by May Swenson
**8** Giving shape to your thoughts II                            48
   'Think of this Tower-block' by Michael Rosen
**9** Words into actions II                                       52
   'Julian' by Ray Jenkins
**10** Beginnings and endings                                     59
   'The End of Something' by Ernest Hemingway
**11** The hidden persuaders                                      65
   Extracts from The *Daily Mail* and *Sunday Mirror*
**12** Alternative versions                                       70
   'First Frost' by Andrei Vosnesensky
**13** Key Questions II                                           72
   'The Bicycle Race' by Michael Anthony
**14** Words into actions III                                     77
   Extract from *City Sugar* by Stephen Poliakoff

**15** Finding your own way into a story     82
'The Use of Force' by William Carlos Williams
**16** Final thoughts: words and pictures     88
'Market Economy' by Marge Piercy
Photograph 'Legs' by Renta Snap

More stories and poems     90

Appendix 1     92
'The Secret in the Cat' by May Swenson (full version)

Appendix 2     94
'The Singer' by Bertolt Brecht

# ACKNOWLEDGEMENTS

The authors and publishers wish to thank the following who have kindly given permission for the use of copyright material:

Associated Book Publishers Ltd for 'City Sugar' from *Hitting Town and City Sugar* by Stephen Poliakoff, published by Methuen London;

Jonathan Cape Ltd for 'First Day at School' from *In the Classroom* by Roger McGough, and on behalf of the Executors of the Ernest Hemingway Estate for 'The End of Something' from *The First Fortynine Stories*;

Andre Deutsch Ltd for 'Think of this Tower-block' from *Wouldn't You Like to Know* by Michael Rosen, and 'The Bicycle Race' by Michael Anthony from *The Games Were Coming*;

Edward Lowbury for his poem 'Prince Kano' in *Green Magic*;

New Directions Publishing Corporation for an extract from *The Farmer's Daughters* Copyright 1938 by William Carlos Williams;

Penguin Books Ltd for extracts from *Basket-Ball Game* by Julius Lester (Peacock Books 1977) Copyright © Julius Lester 1972, and 'The Place' by John Gordon from *The Spitfire Grave and Other Stories* by John Gordon (Kestrel Books 1979) Copyright © 1971, 1973, 1975, 1979 by John Gordon;

Margaret Ramsay Ltd on behalf of Ray Jenkins for an extract from *Julian*;

Vernon Scannell for his poem 'Uncle Albert' from *Mastering the Craft*;

Syndication International Ltd for football reports from the *Sunday Mirror* 10 October 1982;

Wallace & Sheil Agency Inc. on behalf of Marge Piercy for the poem 'Market Economy' from *The Twelve-Spoked Wheel Flashing* published by Alfred A Knopf Inc.

Every effort has been made to trace all the copyright holders but if any have been inadvertently overlooked the publishers will be pleased to make the necessary arrangements at the first opportunity.

The author and publishers wish to acknowledge the following photograph sources:

Ashmolean Museum, Oxford p.39; Daily Mail/British Museum Newspaper Library p.67; Rentasnap Photo Library p.89; Tate Gallery Archives 1072/p — Published by courtesy of the Paul Nash Trust p.36.

The publishers have made every effort to trace copyright holders, but if they have inadvertently overlooked any they will be pleased to make the necessary arrangements at the first opportunity.

# INTRODUCTION FOR TEACHERS

## New approaches to Comprehension — ways of making sense

'In searching for ways and means of improving reading comprehension, it would appear that a prime consideration should be the involvement of pupils in their reading. At the heart of the matter is the willingness to reflect.'

E. Lunzer and K. Gardner, *The Effective Use of Reading*
(Heinemann, 1979 edn)

Read the following passage carefully:

Spring burst upon the Island with exciting suddenness. I don't remember it as a time of slowly unfolding buds and the hesitant stop-start of spring in other parts of the country. There are no hedgerows and trees to creep timidly into leaf and the countryside never has that unsatisfactory piebald appearance with some trees in full fig whilst others remain stubbornly bare and austere.

   As a child spring always started for me on the day when the cattle were let out. All winter they remained chained up in the byre until one magical morning when it was decreed that they could be let out to grass. The field gates were opened and everything cleared from their path. Then their neck chains were loosed and whoever opened the byre door flattened himself against the wall so as not to be trampled underfoot in the first hectic stampede. They rushed through the doors as wild as steers at a rodeo. Matronly milk cows tossed their horns and kicked their heels like frolicsome calves in the fresh air and galloped from end to end of the field, their tails curled high over their backs, bellowing with delight that the long winter months were over.

Then we knew that spring had really come. The crops would soon be sprouting and, for the first time, you noticed that the lady's smocks and the primroses were in full bloom.

Answer as far as possible in your own words:
(a) Is this passage written in the first, second or third person?
(1 mark)
(b) How did the arrival of spring on the Island differ from its arrival in other regions of the country? (2 marks)
(c) When did spring begin for the author when he was a boy?
(2 marks)
(d) What is a byre? (2 marks)
*R.S.A. English Language Paper 1976*

Did you find it difficult to keep your mind on what you were reading? Did the passage make you *want* to understand more of what was going on? If not, then you can probably sympathise with the great number of pupils who, when faced with Comprehension exercises like this in class and in the examination room, react with dutiful blankness.

Dull passages, often ripped out of any real context, are coupled with lists of over-literal or irrelevant questions, written in a confusing language spoken only by seasoned examiners. The frequent result is that a cramped and passive role is forced on even the brightest pupils.

Many of these mechanically applied Comprehension tests have encouraged pupils to jump through rows of teacher-held hoops, but they have not done what they professed to do — that is, they have not actually helped children to improve their understanding skills. Again, the *Effective Use of Reading* team got it right:
'...experienced teachers are aware that children rapidly learn to treat comprehension exercises for what they are: irrelevant chores that one must complete to satisfy someone else.'

Whatever the justifications have been in the past, the move to a national pattern of examining at 16 + and the increased possibilities for a school-based, 'course-work' type of submission mean that it is now both possible, as well as necessary, to adopt a range of much more productive approaches to Comprehension in English.

## But what do we mean by Comprehension?

We are arguing for an active approach to Comprehension in English, as a valuable understanding process in its own right and not simply as an easily quantifiable activity of little worth in itself.

Comprehension is concerned with asking questions and getting answers. All of us, in our daily lives, are continually asking questions, and as long as we receive satisfactory answers, we say that we comprehend. As Frank Smith puts it in *Reading:* 'Teachers often regard comprehension as the result of learning rather than the basis for making sense of anything. So-called comprehension tests are usually given after a book has been read, and as a consequence are more like tests of long-term memory. . . Comprehension is not a quantity, it is a state — a state of not having any unanswered questions.'

Seen in this way Comprehension becomes part of the way we make sense of what we live through generally; of relating new experiences and insights to what is already known.

Comprehension then, through understanding. Understanding through having questions satisfactorily answered. But whose questions? Answered in what ways?

It is here that an important shift is needed — away from teachers interrogating pupils about texts, and towards teachers helping pupils to interrogate texts for themselves.

## How can we implement an active approach to Comprehension in the classroom?

### What kind of texts are needed?

Perhaps the first thing we might do in the classroom is to make a strong case for the quality of the material we put in front of the pupils. We need to replace the *Reader's Digest* style of extract found in much Comprehension work with stories and poems like 'The Use of Force', William Carlos Williams; 'The End of Something', Ernest Hemingway; 'The Secret in the Cat', May Swenson: texts that speak directly and powerfully to the felt preoccupations of this age group. (A selection of suitable stories and poems can be found at the end of this book.)

3

This is not a limited call for parochialism but a cry for immediate, concise material that excites pupils' curiosities about the reasons why people say and do the things they do. As one fifteen-year-old remarked on the qualities of Comprehension passages that interested her, 'I like them if they're intriguing and they have got a lot of emotion in them. To read on you need some emotion or...a relationship with the characters, I think.'

The fragmented state of many extracts, wrenched from their original contexts, does not allow pupils to enter into them as readily as does the more satisfying wholeness of complete stories. With extracts the story logic is often destroyed so that the pupils' emerging expectations, a necessary part of making sense out of what they read, are frustrated. But with more fully developed and tightly shaped stories or extracts that stand by themselves, the pupils' predictions can become an important part of interrogating the text. Furthermore, pupils are usually more positively receptive to complete stories and poems that have an internal consistency and logic, so that they are carried forward with the linked unfolding of the story or poem.

The stories and poems we select need to be recognisable and direct but also potentially puzzling and open to alternative interpretations. The material itself needs to open out and encourage a range of questions, guesses and hunches about possible human intentions, rather than closing things down towards neatly packaged conclusions. It is here that literature, understood in the broadest sense, as opposed to merely informational material, comes into its own.

We stand squarely behind Bob Moy and Mike Raleigh in 'Comprehension, bringing it back alive' *The English Magazine* nos 5 & 6, when they state that:

> It is not that the reading of literary texts involves unique comprehension processes, but that they involve the comprehension processes uniquely well. They require all the work that more purely informational texts do — but more so. They make a virtue of the fact that different readers are necessarily reading 'different' texts by generously inviting different interpretations. And while literary texts are more 'demanding' in that they require more comprehending the paradox is that when properly chosen. . .they are also more accessible into the bargain.

### How best to use these texts?

Our aim is to encourage an engaged concern with the stories, poems and other material under consideration. We are inviting pupils, in effect, to pause, step inside and carefully reflect upon the material. In order to achieve this, any new approach needs to be perceived as being both worthwhile and necessary by the pupils themselves.

In recent years a great quantity of experience in this area has been collected and considered by the Schools Council sponsored 'Effective Use of Reading' project, based in Nottingham. They have been concerned with setting up structures of 'instruction, guidance and reading practice which improves the quality of reflection.' Their latest enquiry, 'Reading for Learning in the Secondary School' (to be published as *Learning From the Written Word,* E. Lunzer and K. Gardner eds., Oliver & Boyd, 1984), argues for a wide range of Directed Activities Related to Texts, or DARTS, as they have come to be known.

DARTS as defined here have a dual aim of teaching a chosen portion of the curriculum in a stimulating and effective manner and at the same time helping pupils to be more independent in reading and studying. Directed Activities are 'so devised as to focus the pupil's attention on the principal ideas in the passage. In the end, one wants the pupils to become more adept at recognising the underlying structure of any passage, to pick out the meat from the inessential frills.' Clearly, the 'Reading for Learning' team are addressing themselves to the use of written texts across the whole subject range here, but the implications for English are obvious.

They go on to suggest that DARTS tend to fall into 'two more or less distinct groups: text reconstruction and text analysis'. Text reconstruction is concerned with pupils working on texts that have been disrupted or modified in some way, usually by the teacher. Text analysis, on the other hand, involves pupils working on original or unmodified texts. Our own summary of the most useful DARTS would include the following. (What follows is by no means a complete list. Further examples can be found in the excellent article by Bob Moy and Mike Raleigh already mentioned, as well as a piece by Mike Taylor and Bill Deller in *New Directions in English Teaching*, ed. A. Adams, 1983.)

## DARTS using modified texts

### 1 Prediction
A narrative is halted at a crucial moment, or series of moments, in order for students to speculate generally on what might happen next, using cues from the presented text.

### 2 Completion
Texts from which key words or phrases have been deleted. Students discuss possible alternatives, opt for a favourite which best conveys the meaning of the piece and then, perhaps, finally compare with the original.

### 3 Sequencing
Students are involved in re-ordering a scrambled text. Useful comparisons can be made with other rearranged versions as well as with the original.

## DARTS using unmodified texts

### 4 Underlining and labelling
Students mark the text in some way to locate significance or pattern. Texts can also be divided into connected segments with appropriate boundaries being suggested and discussed.

### 5 Responding to statements
Students are presented with a range of statements relating to a text. These can be a mixture of fact and opinion, with some being contradictory or controversial. The students then need to decide which statements are most important or appropriate, giving their reasons.

### 6 Listing the main points in a text
Students construct their own lists of points they feel to be important in the text under consideration. They then go on to elect the key points to indicate areas of crucial significance.

### 7 Students asking their own questions
Students devise their own sets of questions, either for the text as a whole or for specific sections within it.

### 8 Visual representation
Varieties of visual presentation can serve to organise information and characterisation, as well as broader themes within the text. There are also possibilities for a more total representation through poster or title-page design.

## 9 Creative summary and paraphrase

Opportunities for rewriting or reconstructing might include the production of a brief newspaper article or news bulletin based on the text. Alternative openings and endings can be considered, as can reordering the text into a new form, for example into a twenty-minute radio play. Similarly, texts can be completely rewritten, say, for a younger audience.

## 10 Role play and improvisation

Students can reconstruct or extend aspects of the text through appropriate improvisation and role play. The emphasis should be on an interrogative, questioning approach.

These suggestions can all be very productive, especially when used in combination. Such procedures represent a sort of preliminary scaffolding, over and through which pupils can begin to enter texts with a certain, often new-found, confidence.

It will be obvious that the approaches suggested in this book have clearly been inspired by, and indeed often stem from, a direct working relationship with the ideas and approaches first put forward within DARTS. We firmly believe that such activities form a necessary foundation for any further development in this area.

However, teachers need to be aware that in a busy classroom strong tendencies exist for frameworks and procedures to take over. It is, unfortunately, all too possible for such activities to degenerate into a series of routine, mechanical tasks, which touch the surface of the text but which fail to link up and probe its most important meanings and implications. This has also been confirmed by Paul Ashton and David Marigold, who were working specifically with poetry, but it applies with equal force when working with stories or plays: 'To be properly effective, activities of this sort (i.e. DARTS) need to be carefully selected and adapted to fit the poem and suit the class; otherwise they can become merely mechanically applied exercises which interfere unhelpfully between reader and text.' (*English Magazine* no.10)

In summary, what we wish to emphasise is the overwhelming need for an active student engagement with complete stories and poems: an engagement, moreover, which combines a *flexibility* of approach and response with a clear *direction* towards some of the organised patterns of meaning in the material under consideration.

7

# Ways of working

## Comprehension in action — an approach to 'The Place' by John Gordon

Without being rigidly prescriptive, we offer the following 'way of working' as one of the most effective approaches to active comprehension. The five steps of this multiple approach have emerged from direct classroom experience over recent years. We feel that the working examples chosen will speak for themselves.

### Step one: asking your own questions

---

**1 Asking Questions**

Homing in through natural curiosities and what we already know

---

After a class reading of 'The Place' by John Gordon (see page 34), a fourth-year mixed ability group were asked to read the story again carefully as individuals, listing all those points they found puzzling, confusing, interesting or important.

These were the questions the three members of the group came up with:

1 'It *must* have been bright.' Why did he say this?
2 'Even if my house is Bluebeard's castle, and all my previous wives are lying there murdered?' Who is Bluebeard and what point is he trying to make about the wives?
3 He says that he has to tell the woman all about it. Tell the woman about *what*?
4 He says he rather likes finding himself on other people's property — why?
5 Why did she run down the avenue?
6 Which avenue did she run down? Surely he would know?
7 Why wasn't he wanted at the funeral?
8 Had she spoken to the others? Who are the others?
9 Why did all their friends just go?
10 Where did he go at the end of the story?
11 Why did she run into the nearest room?
12 What tapped on the glass?

13 She had the same feeling of power and of owning the house when she was locked in — like he did before?
14 The story repeats itself in an eerie way — what's the writer trying to say?

*Karen*

1 The way the story repeats itself — Why did the same events happen in exactly the same way?
2 The setting of the story — there is not much detail about the surroundings, it is concentrated on the conversation.
3 Not much is said about the people themselves or about what happened to the first woman — why?
4 What is supposed to be going on in the house and why aren't the couple inside it?
5 The way in which the man didn't show much feeling or expression for the woman.
6 Why did the man feel that as he stepped through the door the house belonged to him?
7 Why does the telephone ring just as she is calling him back? Is it all part of the house being haunted or is it genuine?
8 Why does one person end up inside and one outside?
9 What is the tapping on the window caused by?
10 Why did both people experience fear when they were inside the room — because all the lights were on and the 'thing' was outside?
11 What made the woman let go of the door when she knew she could prevent history repeating itself?
12 Why had all the guests left?
13 Was her confirmation of the ghost true?

*Elizabeth*

1 What did the place look like?
2 Who or what answered the phone?
3 Why should he want to bring her back?
4 Why did the house come first and why was it so special?
5 Why does the house have all avenues leading from it?
6 Why did the ghost go away?
7 Was the figure after her? And was the figure in the shape of a man or woman?
8 What tapped on the glass?
9 Was his first wife punishing him?
10 Were the footsteps imagination?
11 Why did she say you must have been very afraid?
12 Why was he scared of the dark?

13 Why didn't he know if the lights were bright?
14 Why was she in control?

*Neil*

As we can see, not all these first responses were of equal value. The next step, therefore, requires the pupils to establish a greater sense of balance and discriminating focus.

### Step two: selecting a key question

> **2 Selecting A Key Question**
>
> Sifting and selecting,
> back to the text to sharpen
> up and direct earlier hunches

The group was then asked to read through their list of questions again and to select what seemed to them to be their most important questions: the question that gets closest to the heart of the story: the key question.

These were some of the key questions chosen:

1 Has the house got some kind of force that draws people towards it? (Karen)
2 Why did the same events happen in exactly the same way? (Elizabeth)
3 Why did the house come first and why was it so special? (Neil)
4 Did he want to scare her away? (Peter)
5 Why did the house seem to separate the two people? (Philippa)
6 Did it happen because of people's love and attraction to the house? (Alec)

### Step three: giving shape to our thoughts

> **3 Giving Shape to Our Thoughts**
>
> Constructing 'spider-plans' based
> around the key question
>
> A chance to combine renewed
> speculation with linked patterns
> of understanding

Having chosen their key questions the group was then asked to build up a spider plan based on it. They were asked to start by suggesting a range of *possible* answers to their key question and to organise these visually around their key question in some way. Then, taking each possible answer in turn, they were asked to carry on the network, in terms of 'Now, if this is a possible answer, what new questions should I now ask? And what new answers might flow from those?' And so on.

It was also pointed out that step three could be used as a practical check on step two. For example, if the first key question selected seems unlikely to generate many interesting possibilities, then perhaps it's not so key after all! So, select another one and try that out.

These are some of the spider plans that were produced:

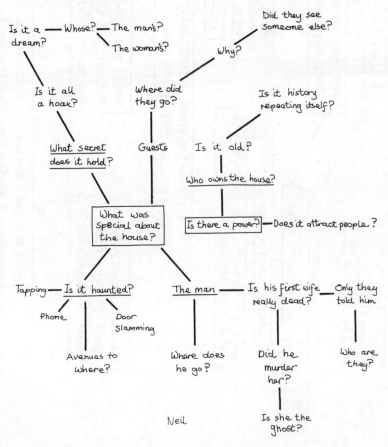

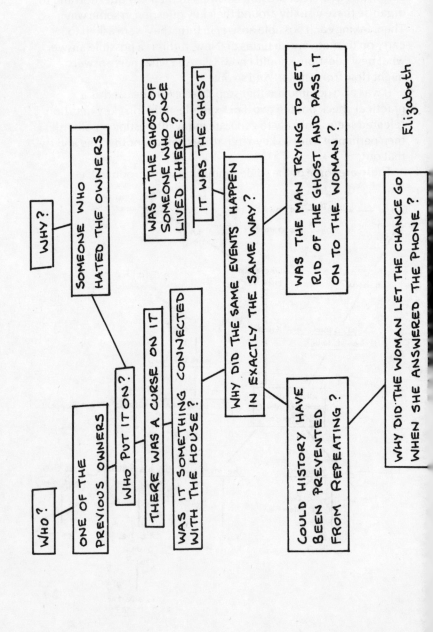

WHY?

SOMEONE WHO HATED THE OWNERS

WAS IT THE GHOST OF SOMEONE WHO ONCE LIVED THERE?

IT WAS THE GHOST

WAS THE MAN TRYING TO GET RID OF THE GHOST AND PASS IT ON TO THE WOMAN?

WHO?

ONE OF THE PREVIOUS OWNERS

WHO PUT IT ON?

THERE WAS A CURSE ON IT

WAS IT SOMETHING CONNECTED WITH THE HOUSE?

WHY DID THE SAME EVENTS HAPPEN IN EXACTLY THE SAME WAY?

COULD HISTORY HAVE BEEN PREVENTED FROM REPEATING?

WHY DID THE WOMAN LET THE CHANCE GO WHEN SHE ANSWERED THE PHONE?

Elizabeth

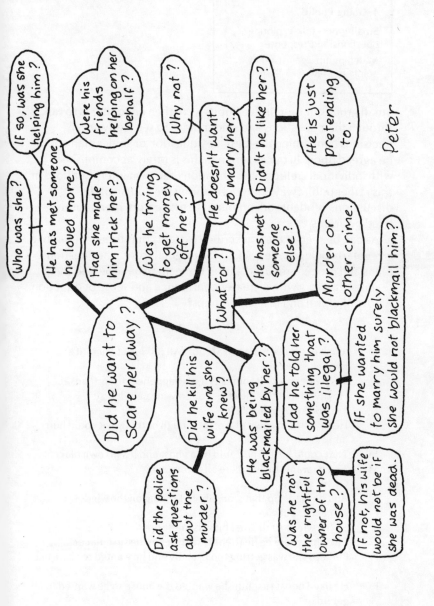

13

## Step four: going public

> **4 Going Public**
>
> Small group talk exploring
> questions and responses
> Matching up against other
> points of view

Small groups of four or five pupils were then encouraged to talk
through their questions and spider plans to see if any group
decisions concerning the 'best' key question or spider plan could
be agreed upon. In our experience this is rarely accomplished,
with individuals reluctant to abandon their own interpretations in
this rather public way. However, during the course of the
discussions, students are prepared to move from prematurely
fixed positions.

As can be seen in the transcribed extracts that follow, reference
is regularly being made back to the original story. The questions,
plans and procedures used earlier do seem to have helped them
re-enter the story with a greater confidence and sense of direction.
A not unhelpful end in itself perhaps?

*A*

| | |
|---|---|
| S | 'One learns not to be too afraid.' (All talking at once): it's happened before. |
| S | Yes it does make it sound as if it's happened often. *(Pause)* |
| F | He says that it has the effect of drawing people to it. |
| F | Yes, lots of people like it. |
| F | He says 'It's my own place,' as though nothing in it could hurt him. |
| M | That could be it. . .he could be a ghost and it's his own place. |
| M | And he wants to live there all on his own? |
| S | On his own? |
| M | And he made up that story about tapping on the window. |
| F | To get her out. |
| S | So the whole of the first bit was made up. |
| F | But why would he be friendly with her in the first place? |
| F | Perhaps she was getting too friendly and he wanted to scare her off. |
| F | He liked her at first but she wanted the house so he wanted to get rid of her. |
| F | Perhaps he didn't like the idea of anyone else having the house. |
| M | That's it. *(Laughter).* |

| | |
|---|---|
| S | So he was being possessive about the house. |
| F | He said he wanted it as well. |
| M | So he won't be a ghost. |
| F | It could be a ghost that wants the house and doesn't want her to have it so he haunts it. |
| D | What do we know about this earlier relationship? |
| F | With his first wife? |
| D | With his first woman. |
| M | It's exactly the same as his second one. |
| S | What would your continuation to the end be? |
| F | She'd probably. . .something else would happen. It would repeat over again — somebody else would come and it would — |
| M | (It'd go back to the start!) Start again — she'd be so scared she'd probably die of shock. |
| S | So she has the house for a while and it repeats again. |
| F | I don't think she'll keep it. I think she'll be too scared. |
| S | What'll happen to him? |
| F | He'll come back. |
| M | He'll die like she did and there'll be no evidence he's died. |
| F | Or he might just die. . .he might haunt it. |
| S | So was it her when he heard the tapping on the window? |
| F | It could have been his ex-wife, the one that's dead. |
| F | She might have come to haunt him. One might be resentful 'cos she doesn't want him to marry anyone else. So she might come back and frighten them off. |
| F | It says here that it was time to go to meet him at the end. |
| F | Yeah, I didn't get that. |
| M | Where's it say that? |
| S | Yes 'cos she'd decided, hadn't she, that she didn't want him to go. She knew it looked as though history was repeating itself. Did anyone else understand that? Anyone think they can explain it? |
| F | She doesn't want the house to herself. |
| F | She wanted to go and see if she could find him. |
| F | I know but she was still 'confused' it says. |
| F | But she hadn't got up then. *(All talking at once)* Something tapped on the window. |
| F | She didn't want the door to close between them. She wanted to keep it open. It was just when the telephone rang she was scared. |
| S | So it's almost as if the house has taken over. |

*B*

1. My question is: What was the attraction of the house, and why was it so. . .and, did the house cause it, and if so, why did it?

15

2. Because it was such a beautiful place — the shape of it was beautiful.

3. I wondered if it was supernatural at times.

1. Or was it the atmosphere?

T. Do you think the author intended there to be just one cut-and-dried answer?
   What are some of the clues you were given?

1. Well, since it was such an old house, it would tend to have an atmosphere.

3. I think it was a supernatural attraction.

2. The supernatural and the atmosphere could be linked. . .The supernatural would tend to affect the atmosphere, wouldn't it?

T. What other clues are you given?

1. These two people say they love each other. . .It doesn't strike me that they love each other.

3. They love the house.

2. Yeah.

1. If they love the place, rather than the other person, it doesn't seem to be a very good preparation for a healthy marriage.

3. One clue might be that the house might actually be separating the people and driving them apart — after living in the house awhile the bloke might come to hate it — I used to be like that — She loves it, and he hates it. . .

3. She seems to be more interested in the property than in him.

2. You don't know what she was like before she knew about the house.

1. Do we know enough about what happened in the first relationship?

2. We don't know whether they were married or were going to marry.

1. I think the house caused the attraction. . .she likes it so much.

3. Maybe it kind of hypnotized her. . .with the supernatural atmosphere.

1. She never had been to the house before, yet she wanted to explore it.


### A word of caution

With this story, the pupils did tend to get sidetracked by the lure of the supernatural (see Elizabeth's references to a 'curse' or a 'ghost' as explanations in her spider plan).

As adults we might pick out other features for our key questions: the hand of the author in structuring the narration; or the nature of the emotional relationship, which is repetitively and almost inevitably destroyed once the possessive urge begins to grow.

The story can obviously be interpreted at different levels, according to age or experience. The strength of this approach is that the story and the questioning method are equally valid at all levels, whereas the straight comprehension question tends to tie the interpretation of the text to one level alone.

### Step five

> **5 Optional Final Stage**
>
> Pupil-teacher negotiation of more formal 'understanding assignment'

A possible final stage, aimed at combining a teacher's need to consider certain, perhaps submerged, implications of the text with the natural curiosities of the pupils, might well be a more formal, concluding assignment.

This sort of response, perhaps coupled with earlier, more independent workings, would also have an obvious relevance for the folder-work requirements Examination Boards are asking for at 16 + .

Students can be asked to respond in writing to a commonly agreed range of 'Understanding' type questions. It is important that such questions should represent the combined reactions of both students and teacher to the text. A genuine dovetailing of interests and curiosities needs to take place if that cramped passivity mentioned earlier is to be avoided. Such Understanding Assignments could also, of course, include the possibility of more sustained writing extensions. What follows is an example of just such a joint undertaking, decided upon after the previous four steps had been completed.

### Understanding Assignment: 'The Place'

1   Using your own words, describe briefly what happened between the man and his first wife. Why might this be important?
2   What incident triggered off the chain of events between the man and the woman for the second time?
3   Look closely at the way the author uses individual words and phrases in the story. How does he manage to build up suspense and create a spooky atmosphere? How successful do you think he is in this?
4   Why do you think the story is called 'The Place'? Try to think of as many reasons as you can.

5    About half way through the story, where the man is describing
     the incident between himself and his first wife, he says: 'I
     suddenly felt in possession of the house — her house.' And a
     little further on, 'It was as though the house wanted me and
     not her.' What do you make of these two sentences?

## Other ways of working

At the outset we mentioned that we did not wish to be 'rigidly
prescriptive' with ways of working, and that the five steps, which
could be represented diagrammatically, are:

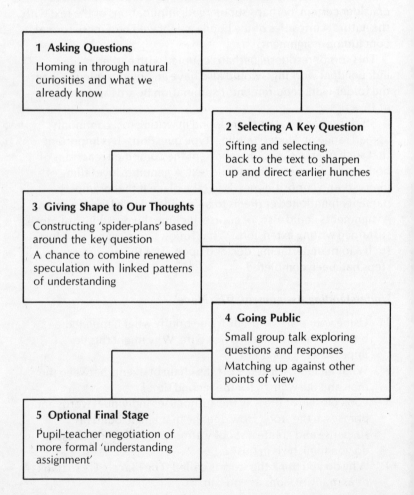

**1  Asking Questions**

Homing in through natural
curiosities and what we
already know

**2  Selecting A Key Question**

Sifting and selecting,
back to the text to sharpen
up and direct earlier hunches

**3  Giving Shape to Our Thoughts**

Constructing 'spider-plans' based
around the key question

A chance to combine renewed
speculation with linked patterns
of understanding

**4  Going Public**

Small group talk exploring
questions and responses

Matching up against other
points of view

**5  Optional Final Stage**

Pupil-teacher negotiation of
more formal 'understanding
assignment'

Whilst being in our experience a particularly effective combination of activities, they are not the only way of encouraging a critical engagement with texts. And whilst we would maintain that the 'five-step' approach could be successfully applied to all the materials presented here, we are also offering a range of other active approaches.

These often relate to activities already contained within the five-step approach, and where they do we have attempted to retain continuity by using a common introductory heading — 'Asking your own questions,' 'Selecting key statements,' or 'Giving shape to our thoughts.'

Where new activities are being suggested, for instance the notions of role play and simulation implied in 'Stepping into the writer's shoes' and 'Words into actions'; the cloze and reverse cloze procedures contained in 'Filling in the gaps' and 'The hidden persuaders'; the possibilities of pictorial interpretation with 'Prince Kano', 'Think of this Tower-block' and 'Market Economy'; the checklist approach leading to small group talk on 'The Library'; the shooting script idea or the two translations of 'First Frost' — these have all been included because they seem to support precisely the kind of flexible yet focused engagement we are trying to develop.

Finally, the order in which the activities and texts occur is not accidental. We are attempting to encourage a growing self-confidence within students, through a familiarisation with a variety of possible approaches to texts, each one as valid as the next. To this end there is a deliberate line of march built into our selection, which starts with such specific tasks as 'Asking your own questions' and which moves, through an accumulating and related set of activities, towards the more general possibilities suggested by 'Finding your own way into a text' at the end of the book.

# 1 ASKING YOUR OWN QUESTIONS

**'Uncle Albert'** *Vernon Scannell*

Read through 'Uncle Albert' as carefully as you can. As you read, whenever you find something *puzzling* or *important* jot it down. By the time you have finished you will have built up a list of your *own* questions on the poem. Remember, don't try to give the teacher what you think she wants but stick to your own hunches.

### UNCLE ALBERT

When I was almost eight years old
My Uncle Albert came to stay:
He wore a watch-chain made of gold
And sometimes he would let me play
With both the chain and gleaming watch,
And though at times I might be rough
He never seemed to bother much.
He smelled of shaving-soap and snuff.
To me he was a kind of God,
Immensely wise and strong and kind,
And so I thought it rather odd
When I came home from school to find
Two strangers, menacing and tall,
In the parlour, looking grim
As Albert − suddenly quite small −
Let them rudely hustle him
Out to where a black car stood
Both Albert and his watch and chain
Disappeared that day for good.
My parents said he'd gone to Spain.

*Vernon Scannell*

You can now go on to consider your list of puzzling or important points in more detail. For instance, do some of your questions seem to be more important than others? If so, underline them — these might be leading you deeper into the poem.

This is the list one fourteen-year-old girl came up with. Don't just copy it. Argue with it. Take it to pieces and decide where you differ.

1   Albert was fantastic in the eyes of his nephew. Perhaps Albert was covering something up and pretending to be very nice.
2   Why did Albert come to stay? Didn't he have his own home or was it best for him to keep moving?
3   'To me he was a kind of God, immensely wise and strong and kind.' Was he really like this or did he just seem this to his eight-year-old nephew? He sounds too nice to be true, as though he was false.
4   The two strangers whom Albert let boss him about: were they the police?
5   'My parents said he'd gone to Spain.' This line sounds as if the young child wasn't sure that he had, as though he believed his parents weren't telling the truth

*Jacqui*

## From another angle: an alternative point of view

In the poem 'Uncle Albert' we see the whole incident through the eyes of the eight-year-old nephew. An interesting possibility would be to re-tell the event from Albert's point of view — either as a story or a poem.

Here is one example. What do you make of it?
Could you do better?

### Albert's Story

It was sad that it had to happen that way, right in front of the kid as well. That was one thing I didn't want to happen. I wasn't going to do anything like that any more, that job had been my last. I really did mean to settle down and go straight this time. But then someone had to go and grass on me. I s'pose I've done one job too many, trusted one person too many. I'd nicked the last car and got my last dishonest money. I'd packed the game in for good. Then I went to my brother's house, to lie low for a while. My brother was pleased with me, he believed I was now straight. He was also pleased I took an interest in the kid, perhaps he thought I might settle down soon and get married myself. I was beginning to believe it, I became more relaxed and began to enjoy myself as an honest man. I enjoyed having the kid around, he was someone who was happy to listen to my stories, easy to please and wasn't spoilt. A very nice young lad. But then the pigs were there, breathing down my neck. They could've at least copped me down the local and not made a scene at my brother's house. I've never been bothered of what people have thought before, but this time I can't help thinking of what the kid thought, running home from school to find the pigs there. Did he know who they were and where I am now? I know he wondered why I let them boss me about, he'd never seen me that way before. And then I was hurried off, without even a goodbye to them. By the time I'm free and have the courage to see them all again, he'll be a man of the world. Perhaps he won't even remember me, perhaps no one will.

*Jacqui*

Whatever happens, you will be trying to make sense of your reactions to the poem in your own way. Remember, you're in charge!

# SELECTING KEY STATEMENTS

**'The Library'** from **Basketball Game** *Julius Lester*

After reading the passage a couple of times, split up into small groups of three or four. Then see if you can agree amongst yourselves which *two* of the statements after the story seem to be *most* important.

## THE LIBRARY

He didn't know how far he walked before he saw a stone building sitting on a hill. That was probably the library. It looked just like the one in Kansas City, gray and ugly. He walked quickly up the steps, studiously ignoring the white faces he passed. He went into the building as if he'd been there many times and walked to the desk. When the old white woman looked up, her jaw dropped. 'What do you want?' she said sharply.

'I'd like to apply for a library card,' he said firmly.

'You can't come to this library,' she said nervously.

Allen could feel his heart pounding as he noticed the white people in the library gathering a short distance away. He didn't know what to do, but he knew he couldn't walk out of that library past all those white faces. He couldn't let them run him away. 'Why not?' he said calmly.

'You just can't,' the old woman said, more agitated. She had lowered her head and was busy stamping some cards on her desk.

'I would take proper care of the books.' He spoke distinctly and evenly, betraying no emotion and being very careful not to sound colored, like his father. And though he was angry, his voice was as pleasant as if he were talking about the weather.

'This is the white library!' the old woman blurted out. 'You people have your own library.'

Allen hadn't known there was a colored library, but it didn't matter.

'But one does not have the wide choice of books there that are available here. And I think it's the duty of all Americans to be as fully educated as they can be. Don't you agree?' He almost burst out laughing and wished his father was there to see him.

The old librarian turned a deep red and refused to answer. When Allen realised that she was going to ignore him he became frightened. He couldn't let her win. He simply couldn't. 'Is there a law against my availing myself of these facilities?'

'Yes,' the woman snapped.

'Might I see it please? I'm not familiar with it.'

'Where you from, boy? ' the woman asked evenly, looking at him through narrowed eyes. 'You don't talk like you from Nashville.'

'No I'm not. I've just moved to the city from Pine Bluff, Arkansas.' And it wasn't a total lie. He had been in Pine Bluff for a week before they came to Nashville. It was obvious, however, that he wasn't going to get a library card. He could sense that a crowd had gathered, and he knew that if he continued to press her something might happen. He didn't know what – she might call the police. But he had to have a library card.

Just then a young white woman came out of a back office. Uh-oh, he thought. The old woman had probably pushed a buzzer under her desk, or somebody went and got this younger one and she was coming out to tell him to leave before she called the cops.

'May I help you?' the woman said pleasantly.

'Yes, I would like to apply for a library card and this woman told me I can't have one. I don't understand why. All I want to do is read.'

'What are you interested in?' the young woman continued.

'Oh,' Allen began eagerly, 'I'd like to see if there's a biography of Winslow Homer. He's one of my favourite painters. And also I'd like the Thayer two-volume biography of Beethoven.' He was sincere, but he was also trying to impress her. She probably thought he was going to list some novels or murder mysteries.

'Well, Mrs Helms,' the younger woman said, 'since I know those books wouldn't be available at the colored library, I don't think we'd be breaking any rules if we let this young man have a card.'

Allen allowed himself to get happy, but the woman had called him 'young man' and not 'boy', and that made him a little wary. No white woman called a Negro anything but 'boy'.

The old librarian was obviously furious, but she only spluttered, 'Whatever you say, Mrs MacIntosh.'

Allen was surprised. The younger librarian was probably in charge of the whole library. The other one probably wasn't even a librarian, but just some ol' white woman who sat there and looked so unpleasant she made people want to read books so they'd forget about her.

'Would you come with me, please?' the younger woman said.

Allen wanted to turn and stick out his tongue at all the white people standing around, but just as he had shown no expression the day he scored twelve points, his face was impassive now. He walked into the woman's office and she handed him a card to fill out.

'These people are funny, aren't they?' she said.

'I beg your pardon?' he replied cautiously.

'I mean their silly rules. They think the library will fall if colored people start using it.'

He didn't say anything, knowing that it was particularly unwise to get into conversations with white people when they were talking against other white people. He filled out the card quickly and handed it back to her.

'You're only fourteen?'

'That's right,' he said pleasantly.

'Aren't you mighty young to be reading such difficult books?'

'I don't think so.'

'Well, we'll have to have your mother or father's permission. Take this card home,' she said, handing him another card, 'and have your mother sign it and bring it back as soon as you can. In the meantime I'll make out a temporary card for you so you can take some books out today. When you bring this other card back with your mother's signature, we'll give you a permanent card.' She sat down at the typewriter and quickly typed out the temporary card. 'I don't know if you know it, but you're the first colored person to use this library.'

'I didn't know.'

'There shouldn't be any trouble though. But this could cost me my job.'

He felt a little guilty.

'I don't think so,' she continued. 'They had me come down here from Ohio to take this job, and I don't think they'll fire me just yet.'

So that was it. She was from the North. He wanted to apologise to her for maybe causing her trouble, but he didn't. He hadn't done anything wrong.

'Let me show you around the library so you'll know where the various books are.'

'Oh that's all right,' he said quickly. 'I can find everything on my own.'

'It's no trouble.'

Allen glumly followed her out the door. The last thing he wanted was to be shown around the library by a young white woman. It was bad enough that he was there. But the librarian didn't notice his discomfort. The library lobby was empty now, Allen was glad to note, and the old woman didn't even look up as they passed her desk. He hardly listened as the librarian took him through the stacks, showing him what books were shelved where. 'Here's that Thayer you wanted,' she said, bending down and taking two thick volumes from a lower shelf and handing them to him.

'Thank you.' He held the books in his hands for a moment. They were dusty, but he lifted them to his nose and inhaled. There was nothing like the smell of old books.

'Do you like Beethoven?' she asked.

'Yes, but I haven't heard that much,' he admitted. He didn't tell her that his real interest in Beethoven was in the fact that he'd read somewhere that when the composer was a boy he was so dark he was called 'Spangy'. Allen wanted to find out if Beethoven was really colored.

'Ah, and here's a book on Winslow Homer.'

He took the book from her, anxious to get out of there and run home to report his adventure.

*Julius Lester*

Here are statements from which you should select the best two.

---

**'The Library': a checklist**

1    Allen's whole approach was both intelligent and effective.
2    The older librarian (Mrs Helms) showed how a lot of white folk in Nashville felt and behaved towards black people.
3    The younger librarian (Mrs MacIntosh) was very good at her job but she didn't really understand how Allen was feeling.
4    Allen would never have behaved as he did had he been with his parents.
5    The author wrote this passage to show what racial prejudice is like.

---

There can be no 'right' or 'wrong' answers here — it all depends on how well you argue your case. It might be an idea to tape record your discussion so that you can compare your ideas with those from other groups later on.

## From another angle: a shooting script

A good way of getting inside a story and really making sense of it is to try to transform it into a shooting script for a film crew.

Firstly you will need to break the piece into a number of distinct scenes. Each scene will need to be described briefly and the camera positions made clear.

To keep your film version visually interesting, you will also need

26

to vary your camera shots, using close-ups and long-range takes.

As an example of what is possible, here is part of a shooting script by Steven, a fourteen-year-old boy, based on the opening paragraphs of 'The Library'. As you will see, not all the dialogue needs to be included — the images can tell a lot of the story for you.

Read it through, then try it for yourself.

### 'The Library': a shooting script

We open with the skyline of Nashville set against a bright blue sky. Long-range shot of the field leading up to the town. Close-up shot of Allen walking briskly to the town. Camera pans to left.

Cut to

*Interior of library*
Medium shot of two ladies. Mrs MacIntosh talking to Mrs Helms.

**Mrs MacIntosh:** Could you go and sort out those books on poetry I was asking for?
**Mrs Helms:** Yes, I put them on one side earlier
**Mrs MacIntosh:** Could you put them on that table please. I'll be in the study room if you need me.

Cut to

*Aerial shot of Allen in streets of Nashville*
Medium aerial shot of Allen, sudden zoom into white face on a nearby doorstep. Fade out and switch to ground shot of Allen, close up on his worried face. Camera pans left and follows him on his brisk confident walk. Follow him around until he is directly in line with the library and camera. Close up of the sign just above the solid oak door, it says 'White Library'. Again zoom in on white faces all watching him confidently walking up the steps.

Cut to

*Interior of library*
Mrs Helms in a medium shot serving a white person. Switch camera angle to slightly behind Mrs Helms with the door in the background, out of focus. When Allen enters change focus so when he takes his first step inside the library he is in focus. Fade him out and switch to a close-up of Mrs Helms' face, her jaw drops. Quick close-ups of all the white people.

**Mrs Helms:** What you want? (Camera pans left to get close-up on Allen)

**Allen:** I'd like to apply for a library card. (Once again the camera focuses on close-ups of white people each looking amazed.)
**Mrs Helms:** You can't come into this library. (Camera swings round to a medium shot of the group of people looking on).

# 3 STEPPING INTO THE WRITER'S SHOES

**'First Day at School'** *Roger McGough*

Sometimes, the best way to understand a poem or story is to try reading it aloud. How exactly should it be read? Why did the writer choose to put it like that? What was he or she trying to get across to the reader?

In small groups, try to decide how best to read this poem aloud to the rest of your group.

## FIRST DAY AT SCHOOL

A millionbillionwillion miles from home
Waiting for the bell to go. (To go where?)
Why are they all so big, other children?
So noisy? So much at home they
must have been born in uniform
Lived all their lives in playgrounds
Spent the years inventing games
that don't let me in. Games
that are rough, that swallow you up.

And the railings.
All round, the railings.
Are they to keep out wolves and monsters?
Things that carry off and eat children?
Things you don't take sweets from?
Perhaps they're to stop us getting out
Running away from the lessins. Lessin.
What does a lessin look like?
Sounds small and slimy.
They keep them in glassrooms.
Whole rooms made out of glass. Imagine.

I wish I could remember my name
Mummy said it would come in useful.
Like wellies. When there's puddles.
Yellowwellies. I wish she was here.
I think my name is sewn on somewhere
perhaps the teacher will read it for me.
Tea-cher. The one who makes the tea.

*Roger McGough*

The different versions and readings should provide you with some new ways of looking at what you think is going on in the poem. Again, it might be useful to keep a tape recorder handy for further discussion or disagreement.

There is actually a tape available of Roger McGough reading the poem himself in *Ways of Talking*, ed. Mike Rosen (Ward Lock Educational). If you can get a copy to listen to, see how his version differs from the one you have arrived at.

To get you going, here is an example of one small group starting to work their way through the poem.

**Teacher:** So how does this show a child's difficulties on his first day in a strange school?

**Chris:** He doesn't know what to expect. . .and doesn't know where to go. . .Would you read it in a slow or fast voice?

**Jane:** Slow.

**Teacher:** Why?

**Chris:** Because he doesn't know anything. . .if you read it in a fast voice you'd feel as if he knows it. . .

**Teacher:** What about the railings bit?

**Mike:** He's sort of locked in. . .

**Ian:** Doesn't know what a lesson is. . .

**Chris:** He doesn't know what it's all about. . .

**Mike:** He thinks the railings are to keep monsters off. . .

**Teacher:** Why might he think of monsters there then?

**Ian:** Because little children have a vivid imagination. . .

**Mike:** Because where he went before. . .where he used to live it was all right. . .and he knew everything but here it could be different. . .and perhaps he never saw school railings before. . . and it's all different. . .

# 4 GIVING SHAPE TO YOUR THOUGHTS I

*'Prince Kano' Edward Lowbury*

Try making sense of 'Prince Kano' visually. You can work by
yourself or in small groups.

Don't rush into it! Give yourself time to re-read the poem
several times, think about it, ask your own questions of it. Make
rough notes on how you can understand the poem by putting it
into picture form. Talk it through in small groups if you like.

## PRINCE KANO

In a dark wood Prince Kano lost his way
And searched in vain through the long summer's day.
At last, when night was near, he came in sight
Of a small clearing filled with yellow light,
And there, bending beside his brazier, stood
A charcoal burner wearing a black hood.
The Prince cried out for joy: 'Good friend, I'll give
What you will ask: guide me to where I live.'
The man pulled back his hood: he had no face –
Where it should be there was an empty space.

Half dead with fear the Prince staggered away,
Rushed blindly through the wood till break of day;
And then he saw a larger clearing, filled
With houses, people, but his soul was chilled,
He looked around for comfort, and his search
Led him inside a small, half-empty church
Where monks prayed, 'Father,' to one he said,
'I've seen a dreadful thing; I am afraid.'

'What did you see, my son?' 'I saw a man
Whose face was like. . .' and, as the Prince began,
The monk drew back his hood and seemed to hiss,
Pointing to where his face should be, 'Like this?'

*Edward Lowbury*

Remember, you are not simply illustrating the poem; you are
investigating some of the meanings of the poem, in visual form.
Together or by yourself select details, lines (or go for a whole
feeling or atmosphere) that you think ought to be included in your
visual.

Think carefully about the right kind of visual for what you want
to do, e.g. your own drawing, collage, strip cartoon or film story-
board. (A story-board is a sequence of pictures and captions where
each drawing represents a shot in a short film sequence. Use
simple outlines if you can't draw. But, as with the shooting-script
idea on page 26, vary your shots and write a running commentary
about what is going on including what the characters are thinking
and saying, underneath each frame.

A collage means arranging different pieces of pictures and
materials together on a sugar-paper background so that the whole
picture makes sense, in your own way, of the poem that you've
just read. Here are some examples of the kinds of things you can
stick on to a collage: coloured wools, tissue paper, cellophane,
buttons, found objects, scraps of material, cut-out photographs
from magazines, your own drawing, cut-out silhouettes etc. You
can create a sequence of events within one picture, as in the first
of the pictures which follow.

Finally, write a short description (to go alongside your visual)
that explains how you were trying to make sense of the poem
through the way you did your visual.

Many approaches and interpretations are possible, using visual
ideas and written explanations. Overleaf you can see what one
group came up with. First the visual pieces, then the written
explanation:

'I took all this as a man lost and confused and couldn't understand why. There were people all around him who should help and wouldn't. The drawing helped me decide all this. I saw the man of splendour first, but then it was him who is in the dark, lost world and not people below him. So my drawing turned into darkness, and the obvious person for help, the preacher of the church, wouldn't give it. I see the prince as a lost and lonely man deprived in life with no friends, no kindliness given to him. I think the poem's message is not to take everything for granted.'

*Jacqui*

'My Prince Kano visual is designed to show both the story and the evilness it is built upon. The centre picture is supposed to show evil things, or scary things and the outer ones various scenes from the poem. The prince shows a feeling from happiness to terror twice in the poem (finding the burner and seeing no face and finding the church and seeing no face to a priest). It is a long summer day (perhaps midsummer) on which bad things might happen, especially in a deep, dark wood. He thinks he can find a friend to help him but instead finds evil. Perhaps the prince would have ignored both burner and priest had he not been in need of help and this may be why evil appears to him?'

*Tim*

'The prince seems to be experiencing something which is absolutely new to him — fear. Being happy before, where he had all he wanted, then getting lost and finding terror. Something he isn't familiar with and not knowing what's going to happen to him. He wants to go home to love, not be lost in a place he doesn't know about, a place that's dark and evil.'

*Louise*

33

# 5 KEY QUESTIONS I

**'The Place'** *John Gordon*

First get to grips with the complete story. You will probably need to read it at least twice, before starting the step by step questioning which follows.

## THE PLACE

'You must have been very afraid,' she said.

'Well I didn't like it much.'

'I should have died.'

'Yes.' He fell silent, and when he resumed he spoke slowly. 'I was too afraid to open the curtains. At least while the light was on in the room. Whatever it was out there could have looked in and seen me and I couldn't have seen it − whatever it was.'

'You could have put the light out.'

'Then I would have had to cross the room in the dark, go right up to the curtain, and. . .'

'Stop. You make me shiver.' She paused. 'Why didn't you go to the phone?'

In spite of the darkness she could see his smile.

'Don't tell me you had forgotten the phone,' she said.

'No, I hadn't forgotten.'

'You are going to tell me the lines had been cut.'

'No. The phone was working.'

'Thank goodness.'

'I heard it ring.'

'Well then.' She let out her breath, relieved.

'The phone is in the hall,' he said.

'Oh, I see. In the dark.'

'No. I told you I'd put on every light in the house. The hall was very bright.' He thought for a moment. 'It must have been bright.'

'Must have been?' she asked. 'Didn't you go out there?'

He spoke as though he had not heard her. 'I'm sure it was bright, because the lights in the room hadn't failed. They didn't even flicker.' He lifted his head and spoke to her again. 'You know what it's like on a windless night in summer with the lights burning. It was all quite calm.'

'Except you.'

'Except me.'

'Who was it ringing?' she said.

'I don't know. I didn't leave the room. Somebody else answered the phone.'

'What a relief!' She was laughing. 'So there *was* somebody else in the house after all.'

He remained silent and her laughter died.

'There *was* somebody else in the house, wasn't there?' she insisted.

'I don't know why I'm telling you this,' he said. 'Not now, just before we are married.'

'Maybe it's a test.' She came closer. 'To see if I love you in spite of all.'

'Even if my house is Bluebeard's castle, and all my previous wives are lying there murdered?'

'Our castle. I fell in love with it before I even knew you.'

He glanced away down the avenue of trees. 'Yes,' he said, 'this place does have that effect. On most people. I was the same. That's why I have to tell you everything about it.' He drew in his breath and let it out like a sigh. 'Everything that I told you earlier is true. The house was empty except for me.'

'But somebody answered the phone.'

'There was a sound like footsteps. Then the phone stopped ringing.'

'Don't go on,' she said. 'Not while we're out here in the dark.'

'All right.'

'All right? You mean you're not going to tell me what happened next?'

'Well you said. . .'

'You've got to!'

He allowed himself to smile again. 'There's not much more to tell. I sat there. There were no more phone calls, no more footsteps. And towards dawn the scratching and tapping at the window stopped altogether. Then I went to bed.'

'To bed?'

He nodded.

'I don't know how you could. I should have fainted. They would have found me white-haired in the morning. Dead or gibbering or something.'

'It's my own place,' he said. 'One learns not to be too afraid.'

'And nothing since?'

'Nothing.'

35

*A photograph of 'The Secret Garden' taken by artist Paul Nash.*

She fell silent, and after a while he said, 'I don't care what happened. It's a beautiful house. I can't wait to live in it. . .with you.'

They were at the end of a long avenue of trees. He put his arm around her waist, and they looked back towards the house.

'Its windows are so small from here,' she said. 'It looks tiny, yet it's a big house. A very big house. And the grounds are huge.'

'I sometimes don't know myself where they end and then I find myself on other people's property. I rather like that.'

'You are odd,' she said. 'When I live here I won't ever want to go outside the boundary.'

'I felt like that, and so did. . .' He broke off. 'I'm sorry.'

'There's no need to be sorry.' She spoke gently. 'I know it was her house. You've told me all that.'

'I was like you,' he said. 'It was the place that attracted me. She may have been living here still if it wasn't for me.'

'No.' She shook her head. 'It was she who ran away. She just left all this – and you. I know it wasn't your fault.'

He said, 'She changed so suddenly. Nothing had happened until that day, and then it was just the smallest of arguments. I can't even remember what it was about. I've tried. I've tried many times to bring it back but it eludes me.'

'I know.' She had heard him speak of it before, but made no effort to stop him. The more he spoke of it the quicker the memory would be, if not obliterated, at least softened.

'She let me go into the house first. She held back because she was angry. And the door closed behind me. I remember how I felt as it shut – it slammed. I hadn't touched it, but it slammed – and I remember suddenly feeling delighted, wanting her to feel that I had slammed it. But more than that. I suddenly felt in possession of the house – her house. But now she was outside, on the other side of the shut door, and the house was mine. It was as though the house wanted me and not her.'

They walked on a few paces nearer the house before he resumed.

'I was, I suppose, slow in opening the door. Just too slow. Just a fragment of a second too slow. And when I did so she had turned and was running away along the avenue.'

'This avenue?'

'I don't know. It may have been.'

'And you never saw her again?'

'No. I waited. Then one day they wrote and told me she had died. They wrote. They did not give me time to reach her. They had had the funeral before I could get there. They had not wanted me. I don't know what she had told them.'

They walked in silence.

'So you came back here,' she said.

'I had to. I love the place.'

'I can't blame you,' she said. 'I would feel the same.'

He stopped and turned towards her. 'So we have no secrets. I have told you everything.'

'I know,' she said.

'And you?' he asked. 'You have no secrets?'

She shook her head. 'And it was afterwards you thought the house was haunted?'

'Just that one night.'

'You were under a great strain.'

'It was after it happened that the place began to feel emptier and emptier. And then you came along.'

'It was the house.' She teased him. 'The house came first.' She looked away. 'These avenues,' she said, 'they all lead straight to the house. How many are there?'

'I've never counted them. And you are mistaken. They are not all straight. Sometimes you lose sight of the house altogether.'

'But not tonight. And the moon is directly over it so we couldn't lose it even if we tried. It really is lovely.'

'But haunted.'

'That was your last secret. But now you've told me so it doesn't matter any more. It's all gone; vanished.' She kissed him. 'Let's get back to the others. We're so far away you can't even hear them.'

'Perhaps everybody's gone. It's late.'

'All the better. I'd like to have it all to myself, and I hate a party that goes on too long.'

'But they're my friends,' he said.

'There's always another day.'

'I want to see them.'

'You don't think they've been frightened away, do you?'

'What makes you say that?'

'Ghosts,' she said.

He shook his head.

'I'm sorry. I shouldn't have made a joke of it. It must have been very frightening.'

He made no response, and she said, 'You must not blame yourself for being afraid. It was bad enough having a ghost outside the house, but to have one inside as well. . .'

'There was only one. The footsteps inside were only the sounds an old house makes. And telephones eventually have to stop ringing. They can't go on for ever. The only ghost was the one outside, trying to get in.'

'But it didn't. And it went away and never came back.'

He seemed not to have heard. 'I should at least have opened the curtains.'

'Why do you blame yourself?'

'I could have learned something. All I had to do was open the curtains. But I was too afraid.'

'You missed nothing, my darling. It was only a tree tapping at the window.'

'There are no trees that close,' he said.

'A creeper?'

He shook his head.

'It was a moth, or something, attracted by the light.' But he was striding on now, and she had to run a pace or two to catch up. He was gazing ahead.

'They've gone,' he said. 'They've all gone!'

Lights burned in every window, laying patches of brightness on the paving of the terrace. There was no car. Not even the sound of a motor in the distance. At the heart of the avenues the house spread its own radiance like a silent star.

'I'm glad,' she said. 'We don't need anybody.'

'They've deserted us.'

'I don't care. We've got it all to ourselves.' She walked across the gravel to where the light from the open door folded itself down the steps and reached out like a carpet to greet her. The hall was beautiful, full of a dazzling light. Within it there were many doors leading to the intricacies of the house itself. The staircase curved away to the momentary darkness of

*The same 'Secret Garden' by Paul Nash, translated into the medium of a painting.*

a landing. There was so much to explore, and now she could do so because it was all hers. She paused on the steps. 'Let's go in together,' she said.

But he had crossed the gravel to gaze into the tunnel of trees into which the cars must have disappeared. He did not answer. A tiny spasm of annoyance at his neglect crossed her mind, and she stepped into the hall alone.

It was then that she saw that history was repeating itself – the quarrel, the drawing apart which put one inside the house and the other outside – and she acted to prevent it.

She held the door to stop it swinging to if a gust of wind should funnel through the house, and she turned to beg him to come with her. But already he was entering the blackness of the avenue. No matter. She was in control. She could decide what happened next. She opened her mouth to call out and bring him back.

At that instant, as though to obliterate any sound she could make, the telephone on the little table behind her began to ring. She started and swung round. The door, reacting to the sudden movement, slid away from her and slammed shut. She reached for the lock, but it was stiff and complicated and as she fumbled at it the phone dinned at her from its perch – like a black goblin, scolding and shrieking.

She left the door and went towards it to silence it. As she moved, a little more of the landing came into view. Matching her, pace for pace, there seemed to be a figure moving towards the head of the stairs. Yet all their guests had gone.

She spun and ran into the nearest room. The second door slammed behind her and she was alone. She remained where she was, her back against the door. Thank god for all the light. She sat down. He was only just outside. He would soon be back. She heard, through the ringing of the phone, his steps in the hall. Then, mercifully, the phone fell silent.

She breathed deeply, twice, and let her head fall forward. In a moment, when her heart steadied, she would get up and go to him.

The hall was quiet now. It must have been the light shining up through the railings of the landing that had persuaded her there was a figure there. She smiled and let her mind explore the hall, and beyond it to the other rooms. They were all bright, empty, and calm. She breathed easier and raised her head. It was time to go to meet him.

She was still sitting when beyond the closed curtains, something tapped on the glass.

*John Gordon*

**Step one: asking your own questions**

As with the poem 'Uncle Albert', read carefully through the story once again, listing all those points you find puzzling, confusing, interesting or important.

**Step two: sifting and selecting**

When considering 'The Library' you were asked to select some ideas and statements as being more important than others. Read through your list of points again and try to select the most important question; the question that gets closest to the heart of the story: the key question.

**Step three: giving shape to your thoughts**

Again this stage will not be totally new to you (see the approach to 'Prince Kano'). Having chosen your key question, try to build up a 'spider plan' based around it. You can do this by placing your key question in the centre of a piece of blank paper. This key question should suggest a whole range of possible answers: arrange these, visually, around the key question. At this stage your page might look something like this:

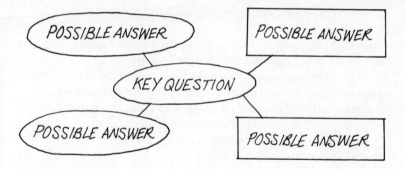

Now take each possible answer in turn and ask yourself the question, 'If this is a possible answer then what *new questions* could I now ask? And what *new answers* and *possibilities* might flow from those?' and so on, and so on.

Each line of enquiry should start to build up a connected web of thoughts, away from the starting point of the key question. Your page could now look something like this:

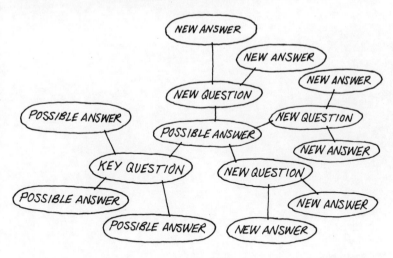

As you work around your possible answers you will find some that are much more fruitful than others. This is only to be expected, and you would do best to concentrate on these.

If you are finding it difficult to come up with many helpful answers or possibilities, perhaps your original question wasn't so key after all! So select another one and try that out. Real dead-ends should send you back to the story for another look.

## Step four: going public

Now that you have your list of questions and your spider plan, why not try them out against other people's ideas?

In small groups, talk through the reasons that led you to select your key question and build up your spider plan. How does it compare with the others? Is it possible to come to a group decision as to the *most effective* key question and spider plan?

How has all this discussion helped you to make more sense of the original story?

# 6 WORDS INTO ACTIONS I

**'Poem for my sister'** *Liz Lochhead*

Start by considering the poem carefully. You may need to ask your
own questions of it, or to work through any of the approaches you
have found useful before.

## POEM FOR MY SISTER

My little sister likes to try my shoes,
to strut in them,
admire her spindle-thin twelve-year-old legs
in this season's styles.
She says they fit her perfectly,
but wobbles
on their high heels, they're
hard to balance.

I like to watch my little sister
playing hopscotch, admire the neat hops-and-skips of her,
their quick peck,
never-missing their mark, not
over-stepping the line.
She is competent at peever.

I try to warn my little sister
about unsuitable shoes,
point out my own distorted feet, the callouses,
odd patches of hard skin.
I should not like to see her
in my shoes.
I wish she could stay
sure footed,
   sensibly shod.

*Liz Lochhead*

In small groups (always basing your talk and actions on what you've just read), try to act out a conversation between big sister and little sister in one of these settings:

Preparing for a disco

Sharing a bedroom

Shopping for clothes on a Saturday

Sunday night at home getting ready for school on Monday

Any other setting that you would like to explore in your own way

You may need to improve the conversation several times before you are happy with the end result. Here is one possibility to help you get started.

### Preparing for a disco

**Little sister:** Hey Jane, can I wear your red shoes tonight?

**Big sister:** Oh Anne, you know you can't walk in them. Anyway they look ridiculous.

**Little sister:** Well, you wear them, and I've been practising walking in them all day. I don't wobble any more!

**Big sister:** You'll be crippled by the end of the night. And how are you going to dance in them?

**Little sister:** I'll take them off to dance.

**Big sister:** Oh yeah, get them stolen or lost.

**Little sister:** Don't be stupid, who would pinch them?

**Big sister:** You're not going to wear them, they're too old for you, just like that make-up. It makes your eyes look like coal pits.

**Little sister:** I did it the same as yours.

**Big sister:** Look, why don't you wear that pretty dress and sandals, they would be more practical and. . ?

**Little sister:** Practical, I don't want to be practical! Won't you ever let me grow up! You wore make-up and high heels at my age, why can't I? You're always wanting me to look like a little baby.

**Big sister:** I just don't want you to make the same mistakes I did. Don't wish your life away, stay young and pure. Don't turn out like me.

**Little sister:** But I want to be like you.

**Big sister:** No! Don't you understand!

**Little sister:** I do, I understand! You want me to wear frilly dresses and sandals all my life. You're just like Mother, so protective. I'm the darling little girl who does everything right. I'm twelve almost thirteen, not a baby any more and you don't understand that, do you?

**Big sister:**    Wear the damn shoes if you have to, cripple yourself, ruin your feet, but don't come running to me. One day you'll realise, and regret it.

*Kate*

Your final version could provide you with the basis for a new piece of writing of your own, either as a story or a poem, in which you could examine conflicts between sisters or brothers in a way that most interests you.

# 7 FILLING IN THE GAPS

**'The Secret in the Cat'** *May Swenson*

There are five missing words in this poem by May Swenson. What might they be? First get a feel of the whole poem before you start suggesting appropriate words.

## THE SECRET IN THE CAT

I took my cat apart
to see what made him purr.
Like an electric clock
or like the ——

of a warming kettle,
something fizzled and sizzled in him.
Was he a soft car,
the engine bubbling sound?

Was there a wire beneath his fur,
or humming —— ?
I undid his throat.
Within was no stir.

I opened up his chest
as though it were a ——
no whisk or rattle there.
I lifted off his skull:

no hiss or murmur.
I halved his little belly
but found no gear,
no cause for static.

So I replaced his lid,
laced his little gut.
His heart into his vest I slid
and buttoned up his throat.

His tail rose to a rod
and beckoned to the air.
Some —— made him vibrate
warmer than before.

Whiskers and a tail:
perhaps they caught
some radar code
emitted as a pip, a dot-and-dash

of woollen sound.
My cat a kind of tuning fork? –
amplifier? ——? –
doing secret signal work?

His eyes elliptic tubes:
there's a message in his stare.
I stroke him
but cannot find the dial.

*May Swenson*


Remember, there are no 'right' answers here. What matters is
whether you can produce good reasons for your own gap-fillers, in
terms of meaning, sound, context etc.

If you are unsure how to start, list several possibilities for each
gap, and then after thinking about them underline your favourite.
Also, see how your ideas compare with others in your group.

# 8 GIVING SHAPE TO YOUR THOUGHTS II

**'Think of this Tower-block'** *Michael Rosen*

As with 'Prince Kano', this poem by Michael Rosen lends itself well to a visual treatment. First read the poem, thinking of the visual images it suggests to you.

### THINK OF THIS TOWER-BLOCK

Think of this tower-block
as if it was a street standing up
and instead of toing and froing
in buses and cars
you up and down it
in a high speed lift.

There will be no pavement artists of course
because there aren't any pavements.
There isn't room for a market
but then there isn't room for cars.
No cars: no accidents
but don't lean
out of the windows
don't play in the lifts
or they won't work.
They don't work
and they won't work
if you play Split Kipper,
Fox and Chickens, Dittyback,
Keek-bogle, Jackerback,
Huckey-buck, Hotchie-pig,
Foggy-plonks, Ching Chang Cholly
or Bunky-Bean Bam-Bye.

Go down. The stairs are outside –
you can't miss them – try not to miss them, please.
No pets.
Think how unhappy they'd be
locked in a tower-block.
There will be
no buskers, no hawkers
no flowers, no chinwaggers
no sandwich boards,
no passers-by,
except for
low-flying aircraft
or high-flying sparrows.

Here is a note from Head Office:
you will love your neighbour
left right above below
so no music, creaky boots,
caterwauling somersaulting –
never never never jump up or down
or you may
never never never get down or up again.
No questions.
It's best to tip-toe,
creep, crawl, and whisper.
If there are any
problems phone me
and I'll be out.
Good day.

*Michael Rosen*

One idea for your visual treatment might be to see what you can
make of it as a cartoon strip.

The examples on the following pages might help you on your
way.

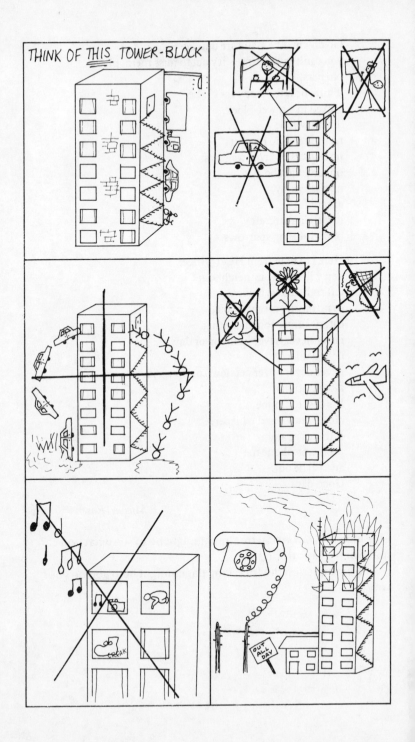

# 9 WORDS INTO ACTIONS II

*'Julian' by Ray Jenkins*

You can approach this drama exercise in a similar way to 'Poem for my Sister'. First make as much sense of the play extract as you can. (You may need to read and perform it through several times. as well as asking your own questions, discussing it in small groups etc.)

## JULIAN

(The play takes place in an empty, abandoned church and centres on a dare contest for the leadership of a gang between a supposed softy called Julian and the present leader called Finch who is insecure and apparently hardboiled. Julian wins the dare and takes over the gang by ruthlessly being prepared to break the church's stained glass windows in honour of those soldiers who were killed in the two world wars, while Finch is unable to carry out Julian's dare for him – killing a baby tortoise.)

**Julian:** Hey!
**Finch:** Hey!
**Julian:** Where are you?
**Finch:** Behind you!

   *(A short scuffle of heels.)*

**Julian:** (Calmly) Finch.
**Finch:** Ju-li-an.

   *(Pause.)*

**Julian:** D'you mind not shining that thing in my eyes. . .
**Finch:** Three batteries.
**Julian:** It hurts.

**Finch:** Good.

*(Pause.)*

**Julian:** Why've you locked that door?
**Finch:** I didn't.
**Julian:** Well, one of your 'accomplices'.
**Finch:** 'Accomplices' – big-big words!
**Julian:** Tell him to open it.
**Finch:** Why?
**Julian:** Because I said.
**Finch:** And what will you do if I don't – Lady Muck?
**Julian:** I'll think of something.
**Finch:** Start thinking!
**Julian:** Do you really want to get hurt?
**Finch:** You and whose army?
**Julian:** Me.
**Finch:** Try!

*(A sudden movement, fight, the light falls to the floor.)*

Everybody out!!

*(Plenty of steps and noise.)*

**Julian:** *(Held)* Leave go. . .get these monkeys off my back!
**Finch:** Gor – you're a monkey – Bri you're a chimpanzee! Remember that! *(Breathless)* Down!

*(Julian falls to the floor.)*

Let him go!

*(Pause.)*

Get up. Julie-Anne!
**Julian:** *(Rising)* You can't fight without girls helping!
**Sandra:** I didn't do nothing!
**Finch:** Shut up!
**Julian:** Manners!

*(Half-stifled laughs from the others.)*

**Finch:** Shut up!

*(Silence.)*

**Julian:** Manners, Finchy.

*(Silence.)*

53

**Finch:** You're on trial, kid.
**Julian:** You're mad.
**Finch:** You stink − so we're equal.
**Julian:** I'm going.
**Finch:** You can't get out. . .till we says.
**Julian:** *(Angry)* You trying to −
**Gordon:** We locked the door − thas why.
**Brian:** Try it!

*(Silence.)*

**Finch:** He's thinking − you can hear the little wheels go round!
   You staying then?
**Julian:** *(Mock-calm)* Why not?
**Dave:** We ain't going to −
**Julian:** Hurt me? You couldn't.
**Dave:** It's like − a game −
**Julian:** Good, I like games.
**Finch:** *(Harsh)* Sit down!

*(Pause.)*

   Sit down! Your ears blocked?
**Julian:** Thanks.

*(He sits.)*

   Why don't the. . .rest of you. . .make yourselves at home.
**Finch:** Joker!
**Julian:** I mean − all friends together.
**Finch:** Stay on that door Bri!
**Julian:** And you Gordon − *(Mocking)* I might run away.
**Finch:** You hold the torch, Sandy.
**Sandra:** No!
**Finch:** Dave!
**Dave:** Hold it, San −
**Julian:** Tch-tch!
**Finch:** Why don't you shut up!
**Julian:** Manners.

*(Silence.)*

**Finch:** Right, Julie-Anne − Court in Session.
**Julian:** Silence in Court!
**Finch:** Right Dave.
**Julian:** He's the judge!

**Finch:** And I'm the executioner — any odds?

**Dave:** O.K.?

**Julian:** Blimey.

**Dave:** *(Official)* Are you afraid of nothing?

**Julian:** I'm afraid of 'something' — bad English!

**Finch:** Answer him.

*(Pause.)*

**Julian:** I'm afraid. . .yes, sometimes.

**Dave:** What of?

**Julian:** Find out.

**Finch:** We will.

**Dave:** Finch ain't afraid of nothing, are you Finchey?

**Finch:** Shut up.

**Julian:** Manners!

**Finch:** You say that again and you'll be facing the wrong way from your feet!

**Julian:** Go on then.

*(He rises.)*

**Julian:** *(Hard)* Try it. On your own. If you got me in for a fight — let's fight.

*(Pause.)*

**Finch:** Or dare?

**Julian:** Me and you?

*(Pause.)*

**Finch:** O.K.

*(Pause.)*

**Julian:** *(Gently)* Just a game then.

**Finch:** *(Softly)* Truth and dare.

**Julian:** Me and you.

**Finch:** O.K.

**Julian:** I'll do what you want — you do what I want.

*(Pause.)*

**Finch:** O.K.

**Julian:** See who's the boss.

*(Steps.)*

**Ally:** Sandra!

**Sandra:** Shut up.
**Julian:** Tch-tch manners!
**Sandra:** He's a record got stuck!
**Ally:** My tortoise. . .*(Troubled)* gone to sleep.
**Dave:** *(Whispering)* Well don't wake him up then.
**Ally:** *(Whispering)* He's all quiet!
**Dave:** *(Whispering)* Then why don't you go home!!
**Sandra:** The doors're shut!
**Julian:** Heads you say − tails me.
**Finch:** Heads you − tails me.
**Julian:** O.K.

*(A coin spins and stops.)*

Tails. All right − what you want me to do?
**Finch:** Break them coloured windows.
**Sandra:** No!

*(Pause.)*

**Finch:** All of 'em.

*(Pause.)*

*(Triumphant)* What are you waiting for?
**Dave:** Look, Finch −
**Finch:** Scared?
**Dave:** Finch −
**Finch:** Julie-Anne? What are you waiting for little girl?
**Julian:** I'M LOOKING FOR STONES!!

*(Pause.)*

**Finch:** By your foot. Shine the torch, Sandy.

*(Pause.)*

Lots of little stones, see!
**Julian:** What if I don't.
**Finch:** I'm the boss.
**Julian:** And that's what you want.
**Finch:** That's what I want. Scared?

*(Pause.)*

**Dave:** *(Scared)* Ally, come here! And you Sandy.
**Sandra:** Don't break the windows! Stop him Dave!
**Dave:** I ain't doing nothing!

**Sandra:** They belongs to the War! And the names!

*(Pause.)*

**Julian:** O.K.

*Stones are thrown, some miss, some break glass. . .Julian breathes hard, moaning slightly as he throws. Some miss, some hit. Then silence.*

Now do you feel good?

*(Pause.)*

Eh?

**Finch:** *(Awed)* I – I didn't think. . .you had the guts. You done it!

**Julian:** *(Mocking)* Well, I 'got the guts' en I!

*(Pause.)*

*Ray Jenkins*

Now in groups of three or four, take it in turns to put yourselves in the position of either Julian or Finch. The other members of the group can then question you about the reasons for your actions and things you have said as if you really are those characters. You need to answer their queries in role, by trying to imagine how Julian or Finch would have responded, had they been in your shoes.

Only choose a character you feel strongly about. Don't be too soft; hard questioning always produces the most interesting replies!

This is an example of a boy, Sam, being questioned as Finch, the fallen leader.

**Questioner:** Why did you choose the church?

**Sam:** Because it was a quiet place and nobody else could see – nobody could come and interrupt us. . .

**Questioner:** See what?

**Sam:** The fight.

**Questioner:** Were you going to get him?

**Sam:** We were going to see.

**Questioner:** Why did you want to fight him?

**Sam:** Because he was getting on my nerves. . .he was about to take the gang off me. . .

**Questioner:** How d'you work that out?

**Sam:** Because he was only thinking. . .he was really big. . .making a big head of himself. . .everybody was suddenly beginning to like him. . .so I thought I'd better do something about it.

**Questioner:** Did you trust your friends? *(Laughter)*

**Sam:** Yeah, but he might have put them off me.

**Questioner:** Did it worry you that you might not be the leader of the gang?

**Sam:** Yeah. . .because it was sort of. . .my pride. . .sort of thing. . .

**Questioner:** Was it important to you?

**Sam:** Yeah.

**Questioner:** Haven't you got any other friends then?

**Sam:** Yeah, course I have. . .

**Questioner:** Why are you bothered then. . .I wouldn't be bothered. . .

**Sam:** Because they were my best friends.

**Questioner:** Why can't you just share the gang?

**Sam:** Because I don't like him. . .he's one of my enemies.

**Questioner:** Why don't you all go together?

**Sam:** You've just asked me that.

**Questioner:** Why didn't you kill the tortoise?. . .to prove that you were a big head?

**Sam:** Doesn't mean to prove that I'm a big head. . .

**Questioner:** All right then. . .to prove that you were the best?

**Sam:** Because I'm not going to go round killing live things. . .just for that. . .

**Questioner:** Well, Julian would have done. . .

**Sam:** I know he would have done. . .because he doesn't care. . .

**Questioner:** Well! Leaders probably don't care. . .they're not meant to care. . .

**Sam:** Yes they are.

# BEGINNINGS AND ENDINGS

**'The End of Something'** *Ernest Hemingway*

This story by Ernest Hemingway presents the reader with a lot of problems to sort out. How should those conversations between Marjorie and Nick be read? What tone of voice should a reader adopt? Hemingway hardly gives the game away! He hints and suggests a possible reading but we have to decide for ourselves. What do you think?

As with the poem 'First Day at School', you will probably need to tape several alternative versions and talk it through until you decide on the most effective reading — the reading that makes most sense to you, and seems to fit in most closely with what you think the writer was trying to say in the story.

Could you give your reasons for this final choice?

## THE END OF SOMETHING

In the old days Hortons Bay was a lumbering town. No one who lived in it was out of sound of the big saws in the mill by the lake. Then one year there were no more logs to make lumber. The lumber schooners came into the bay and were loaded with the cut of the mill that stood stacked in the yard. All the piles of lumber were carried away. The big mill building had all its machinery that was removable taken out and hoisted on board one of the schooners by the men who had worked in the mill. The schooner moved out of the bay towards the open lake carrying the two great saws, the travelling carriage that hurled the logs against the revolving, circular saws, and all the rollers, wheels, belts and iron piled on a hull-deep load of lumber. Its open hold covered with canvas and lashed tight, the sails of the schooner filled and it moved out into the open lake, carrying with it everything that had made the mill a mill and Hortons Bay a town.

The one-story bunk houses, the eating-house, the company store, the mill offices and the big mill itself stood deserted in the acres of sawdust that covered the swampy meadow by the shore of the bay.

Ten years later there was nothing of the mill left except the broken white limestone of its foundations showing through the swampy second growth as Nick and Marjorie rowed along the shore. They were trolling along the edge of the channel bank where the bottom dropped off suddenly from sandy shallows to twelve feet of dark water. They were trolling on their way to the point to set night lines for rainbow trout.

'There's our old ruin, Nick,' Marjorie said.

Nick, rowing, looked at the white stone in the green trees.

'There it is,' he said.

'Can you remember when it was a mill?' Marjorie asked.

'I can just remember,' Nick said.

'It seems more like a castle,' Marjorie said.

Nick said nothing, They rowed on out of sight of the mill, following the shore line. Then Nick cut across the bay.

'They aren't striking,' he said.

'No,' Marjorie said. She was intent on the rod all the time they trolled, even when she talked. She loved to fish. She loved to fish with Nick.

Close behind the boat a big trout broke the surface of the water, Nick pulled hard on one oar so the boat would turn and the bait spinning far behind would pass where the trout was feeding. As the trout's back came out of the water the minnows jumped wildly. They sprinkled the surface like a handful of shot thrown into the water. Another trout broke water, feeding on the other side of the boat.

'They're feeding,' Marjorie said.

'But they won't strike,' Nick said.

He rowed the boat around to troll past both the feeding fish, then headed it for the point. Marjorie did not reel in until the boat touched the shore.

They pulled the boat up the beach and Nick lifted out a pail of live perch. The perch swam in the water in the pail. Nick caught three of them with his hands and cut their heads off and skinned them while Marjorie chased with her hands in the bucket, finally caught a perch, cut its head off and skinned it. Nick looked at her fish.

'You don't want to take the ventral fin out,' he said. 'It'll be all right for bait but it's better with the ventral fin in.'

He hooked each of the skinned perch through the tail. There were two hooks attached to a leader on each rod. Then Marjorie rowed the boat out over the channel-bank, holding the line in her teeth, and looking toward Nick, who stood on the shore holding the rod and letting the line run out from the reel.

'That's about right,' he called.

'Should I let it drop?' Marjorie called back, holding the line in her hand.

'Sure. Let it go.' Marjorie dropped the line overboard and watched the baits go down through the water.

She came in with the boat and ran the second line out the same way. Each time Nick set a heavy slab of driftwood across the butt of the rod to hold it solid and propped it up at an angle with a small slab. He reeled in the slack line so the line ran taut out to where the bait rested on the sandy floor of the channel and set the click on the reel. When a trout, feeding on the bottom, took the bait it would run with it, taking line out of the reel in a rush and making the reel sing with the click on.

Marjorie rowed up the point a little way so she would not disturb the line. She pulled hard on the oars and the boat went way up the beach. Little waves came in with it. Marjorie stepped out of the boat and Nick pulled the boat high up the beach.

'What's the matter, Nick?' Marjorie asked.

'I don't know,' Nick said, getting wood for the fire.

They made a fire with driftwood. Marjorie went to the boat and brought a blanket. The evening breeze blew the smoke toward the point, so Marjorie spread the blanket out between the fire and the lake.

Marjorie sat on the blanket with her back to the fire and waited for Nick. He came over and sat down beside her on the blanket. In back of them was the close second-growth timber of the point and in front was the bay with the mouth of Hortons Creek. It was not quite dark. The fire-light went as far as the water. They could both see the two steel rods at an angle over the dark water. The fire glinted on the reels.

Marjorie unpacked the basket of supper.

'I don't feel like eating,' Nick said.

'Come on and eat, Nick.'

'All right.'

They ate without talking, and watched the two rods and the fire-light in the water.

'There's going to be a moon tonight,' said Nick. He looked across the bay to the hills that were beginning to sharpen against the sky. Beyond the hills he knew the moon was coming up.

'I know it,' Marjorie said happily.

'You know everything,' Nick said.

'Oh, Nick, please cut it out! Please, please don't be that way!'

'I can't help it,' Nick said. 'You do. You know everything. That's the trouble. You know you do.'

Marjorie did not say anything.

'I've taught you everything. You know you do. What don't you know, anyway?'

'Oh, shut up,' Marjorie said. 'There comes the moon.'

They sat on the blanket without touching each other and watched the moon rise.

'You don't have to talk silly,' Marjorie said. 'What's really the matter?'

'I don't know.'

'Of course you know.'

'No, I don't.'

'Go on and say it.'

Nick looked at the moon, coming up over the hills.

'It isn't fun any more.'

He was afraid to look at Marjorie. Then he looked at her. She sat there with her back toward him. He looked at her back. 'It isn't fun any more. Not any of it.'

She didn't say anything. He went on. 'I feel as though everything was gone to hell inside of me. I don't know, Marge. I don't know what to say.'

He looked at her back.

'Isn't love any fun?' Marjorie said.

'No,' Nick said. Marjorie stood up. Nick sat there, his head in his hands.

'I'm going to take the boat,' Marjorie called to him. 'You can walk back around the point.'

'All right,' Nick said. 'I'll push the boat off for you.'

'You don't need to,' she said. She was afloat in the boat on the water with the moonlight on it. Nick went back and lay down with his face in the blanket by the fire. He could hear Marjorie rowing on the water.

He lay there for a long time. He lay there while he heard Bill come into the clearing walking around through the woods. He felt Bill coming up to the fire. Bill didn't touch him, either.

'Did she go all right?' Bill said.

'Yes,' Nick said, lying, his face on the blanket.

'Have a scene?'

'No, there wasn't any scene.'

'How do you feel?'

'Oh go away, Bill! Go away for a while.'

Bill selected a sandwich from the lunch basket and walked over to have a look at the rods.

*Ernest Hemingway*

## Beginnings and endings in 'The End of Something'

Beginnings and endings are important in so far as they direct us to consider some of the ways in which incidents or characters are linked. Some of the most intriguing questions about stories can arise from investigating these links.

The beginning and ending of 'The End of Something' are particularly puzzling. Some readers find them very frustrating. Why not try to write your own alternative opening and ending to the story?

You could also include a separate running commentary on your alternatives, giving your reasons for writing them as you did.

First, some examples to start you thinking about the possibilities open to you.

### *Opening*

It was almost three weeks since Marjorie experienced the first fishing with Nick, and the journeys out into the lake now became a routine in her and Nick's relationship. It was a routine she loved to fulfil and take part in. But today it was different, something was the matter with Nick, he seemed far away from her, she wanted to reach out and love him close to her face, but there was something inside her stopped her doing so. She tried not to let him know that she sensed something was wrong, maybe he was just feeling down after yesterday, surely he would get used to not having Bill around.

Marjorie sat in the front of the boat as she always did, facing Nick. She liked to watch him.

Nick was quiet, she tried to make conversation, his replies were short-lived and unenthusiastic, she tried to talk as much as usual, not knowing what difference it would make. All the time Marjorie was pushing one thought to the back of her mind, but she wasn't sure what it was, probably because she didn't want to.

*Commentary:* I tried to write the beginning about Marjorie's feelings, her side of the story. I did the same with the ending but I found it much harder. It was difficult to understand what she was feeling when she rowed away in the boat. Did she hate him? Or love him even more? Or couldn't she understand herself? Or what her feelings were?

*Kate*

### *Opening*

'You lost' laughed Bill.
'What are you going to make me do then?' asked Nick dejectedly.
'I dare you to chuck your girlfriend.'
'I c...can't, y...you can't...'

'You can't back out now. I'll name the place and the time all right.'
'I suppose so.'
'O.K., the old ruin, at dusk, you can be doing some fishing.'

*Commentary:* I Made the alternative beginning with the dare. Also the fact that Bill knew where Nick was, and also that Nick wasn't surprised to see him. It says that he (Nick) lay there while he heard Bill come into the clearing. . .how did Nick know it was Bill? It could have been anyone. This enforced my theory about it being a dare.

*Veronica*

### Ending

As they sat on the blanket in silence Marjorie made the decision — 'If he's not going to tell me off his own back I'll make him.'

'Nick, it's over, isn't it, you don't want to see me any more.' He turned away from her wanting to hide his face, ashamed to look at her.

'Yes, Marjorie, it is, I'm sorry but it isn't working out any more, is it?'

There was a pause as Marjorie took in what Nick had said. Isn't working, he says, but it could do, it could be as great as it was before.

'We could try again,' Nick said. 'But it wouldn't work, I know it. None of it's your fault though, it's all mine.'

'Is there someone else?'

'No, not as such but. . .'

'Goodbye Nick!' Marjorie got up, walked down the beach and began to pull the boat out — 'I don't need him,' she thought. 'Not now, not ever.'

As she rowed off towards the Mill, she turned to have one last look. Just in time to see Bill come out of the trees to join Nick.

*Commentary:* Marjorie is filled with hate for Nick. She despises him because he is bringing an end to their relationship. But deep down she really cares about him and regrets that she can't do anything to win him back. Her hate is shown in her first decision of my ending, and then her true feelings show through when she thinks that it could be as good as before.

Nick is disgusted at himself, for having to finish with Marjorie under these circumstances, and wishes that it could be different. He wants to tell her the real reason and is about to tell her but doesn't carry it out.

When she turned to see Bill, she realised the real truth.

*Sarah*

# THE HIDDEN PERSUADERS

*Daily Mail* and *Sunday Mirror*

What will be suggested now is really the reverse of the 'fill in the gaps' type of approach used with 'The Secret in the Cat'. There you were concerned with *adding* certain words in order to complete the sense or meaning of a piece of writing. Here, we shall be involved in *removing* most of the print, leaving only certain key words or phrases.

The words you will choose to leave should provide a sort of *skeletal message,* around which the rest of the article fits.

An example of this kind of exercise is the *Daily Mail* front page (see overleaf). This has been reduced down to just a few important words but somehow the message remains, loud and clear.

Try this technique on the football reports from the *Sunday Mirror* on pages 68 – 9. Reduce them to the bare bones of their meaning, by copying out the key words. Can you spot any patterns emerging?

Compare your 'skeletal messages' with others from your group. Talk through some of the implications. Would this approach work with other stories from the newspapers? Try it out for yourself.

# Daily  Mail

MONDAY AUGUST 15 1977

# DEFEND

CARVING knife honed to razor sharpness
metal pipe       wickedly lacerating
                          grimly
                      murderous

weaponry
Bloody Saturday
                 regalia of hate. Hate
    authority    law + order

    anger     decent
              racist
    acid   knife  assault
    bludgeon
    evil    scar
    slash   fear
    panic      bleeding
Gashed, bruised

    ominous  action

repellent
            racially    paranoia
                            thuggery-
                          revolutionaries
target
troopers    storm-
            savage unscrupulous
ammonia  bleeding  confront

                        complaints
vicious  confrontation
injured                terrifingly
        provocation
    ammonia              brave men
Knives                  wage war
                    Knife  acid
    menace             justice
             punished  severity.
                severity.
alien   riot    law

> Extremist's
>
> danger
>
> shields of freedom

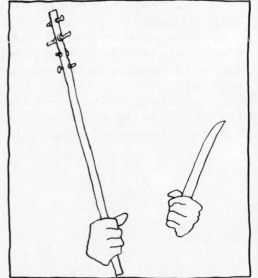

Weaponry    hate    studded club
carving Knife

66

**PETER COOK PAGE 20**

---

## Daily Mail COMMENT

### After the Battle of Lewisham, a question of vital importance

# NOW WHO WILL DEFEND HIM?

...WING knife, honed to razor sharpness. ...etal pipe, with wickedly lacerating ... These exhibits, held grimly aloft by ...don bobby, come from the murderous ...nry deployed against the police on ...y Saturday.

...y are the regalia of hate. Hate for the police, ...hority, for law and order and liberties en-... within that order.

...no honest, spon-...anger by decent ...gainst a racist

...contrived assault, ...and knife and brick ...eon on the police : ... and premeditated ...to scar authority, ...rty and engender ... fear in an already ...ommunity.

...tused and bleeding, ...police held the front ...reedom.

...not seen rougher nor ...rious action since the

...g the right of the ...National Front to ...rough the racially ...areas of Lewisham ...ord, they presented ... as the prime ...y the Red storm-...f the Left

... bags of flour and ...nd jeers they had to ...lime. It was blinding ...and caustic soda.

...m BBC radio, a ...he Socialist Workers' ...bed in the meaning ...clous confrontation ...more than 50 police-...ed It was all the ...he police, he said, ...as the provocation.

...mmonia ? And the ...le refused, though ...challenged, to con-...e use.

...ugust 13, 1977, is a ...menace and signifi-...who value the Bri-...f life should mis-...

...not just the police ...hole of society was ...take shelter behind ...alien looking riot

The police are our shield against the paranoia and thuggery of back street revolutionaries.

Now, we have seen more clearly than ever just what they are defending us against, and how savage and unscrupulous the forces are that they have to confront for our sake.

For too long we have taken them for granted. Turned a deaf ear to their complaints over pay and manning. Walked by quickly on the other side of the road when they needed our help.

It is late, terrifyingly late, for them and for us. We must back our police. We have to support them. We have to pay these brave men what they're worth.

As for those who wage war with the knife and the acid bottle against the police and against our liberties, they must be brought to justice and punished with the fullest deterrent severity that the law allows.

The nation must look to its defences. And that means looking to the police.

### Callaghan intervenes —Page TWO
### Extremists' challenge —Page THREE
### The dangers, by Lord Hailsham—Page SIX
### The shields of freedom Centre Pages

**The weaponry of hate: A studded club and a carving knife used against the police**

*Picture : BILL ORCHARD*

INSIDE : Femail 12, Diary 15, TV 18-19, Letters, Stars, Strips 22, City 23, Antiques 25, Prize Crossword, Theatre Guide 26

# OWEN'S AN AVENGER

West Brom 2    Forest 1

Forest took less than four minutes to hit Albion with a reminder of their nightmare midweek result in the Milk Cup.

Keeper Mark Grew, beaten six times against Forest on Wednesday, failed to hold a header from Ian Wallace and put Albion's revenge plans seemingly on the rocks.

But the game went sour for Forest when referee Eric Read sent off Stephen Hodge in the 27th minute.

The skilful Romeo Zonderman was in full flight over the halfway line when hauled down by Hodge who got instant marching orders.

His loss put Forest on the rack. At one stage they were down to nine men in a five-minute spell when Colin Todd required treatment.

Cyrille Regis smashed home the equaliser in the 36th minute with Forest stationary claiming offside.

Tempers flared with bookings for Albion's Robertson, Regis and Jol and Forest's Wallace and Walsh.

Forest fought to hang on. A one-man rescue operation by keeper Hans van Breukelen in the final half hour denied Albion.

But they took the lead with a brilliant banana shot from 25 yards by Gary Owen in the 60th minute.

As Nottingham's security slowly crumpled Albion's forwards took it in turn to try and beat Breukelen again.

He clipped an Ally Brown shot round the post with an incredible reflex save.

A stunning left foot rocket from Regis was smothered by the super Dutchman and the treatment was just the same for Nicky Cross when he looked certain to score.

Man of the Match: HANS VAN BREUKELEN (Forest).

# ALVIN THE AXE MAN!

West Ham 3   Liverpool 1

West Ham ko'd the champions with three lethal right crosses – and underlined their own claims as genuine title contenders.

Big Alvin Martin – a lifelong Liverpool fan – struck the first hammer blow against his home town heroes in this top of the table thriller.

But it was those lively Londoners, Paul Goddard and Alan Devonshire, who did most to send the Kings of the Kop crashing off the top of the table.

Goddard and Ray Stewart combined sweetly on the right wing, Jimmy Neighbour hit a cross on the run and Bruce Grobbelaar pushed it straight to Martin in the 36th minute. The big England centre half gratefully side-footed the opening goal.

Some superb right wing skills two minutes after the break by Goddard ended with another cross and an equally brilliant left-foot volley by Geoff Pike to put Hammers 2-0 ahead.

West Ham were forced to replace skipper Billy Bonds with Neil Orr and it upset them at the back.

And when Graeme Souness crashed a 25-yard shot past Parkes, we expected yet another of those now famous Liverpool revivals.

But West Ham are made of sterner stuff these days. Off they raced to the other end, once again it was Goddard who produced the right cross and this time Sandy Clark steered the ball home.

Liverpool pushed on sub Craig Johnston for full back Alan Kennedy and staged their usual furious finale.

But with Martin in England form at the back, Devonshire dazzling in midfield and Goddard giving the Anfield defence headaches every time he had control, there was no way that even they were going to come back off the canvas.

Man of the Match: PAUL GODDARD (West Ham).

# 12 ALTERNATIVE VERSIONS

*'First Frost'* Andrei Voznesensky

The two versions of the poem which follows are based on the same Russian poem. The two translators obviously had to make choices as they were searching for the most telling English words.

Read them aloud several times — taking it in turns in a small group.

## FIRST FROST

A girl is freezing in a telephone booth,
huddled in her flimsy coat,
her face stained by tears
and smeared with lipstick.

She breathes on her thin little fingers.
Fingers like ice. Glass beads in her ears.

She has to beat her way back alone
down the icy street.

First Frost. A beginning of losses.
The first frost of telephone phrases.

It is the start of winter glittering on her cheek,
the first frost of having been hurt.

*Andrei Voznesensky*
*translated from the Russian by*
*Stanley Kunitz*

## FIRST ICE

A girl freezes in a telephone booth.
In her draughty overcoat she hides
A face all smeared
In tears and lipstick.

She breathes on her thin palms.
Her fingers are icy. She wears earrings.

She'll have to go home alone, alone,
Along the icy street.

First ice. It is the first time.
The first ice of telephone phrases.

Frozen tears glitter on her cheeks –
The first ice of human hurt.

*Andrei Voznesensky*
*translated from the Russian by*
*George Rearey*

Now make a list of the most important differences; for example
'Glass beads in her ears'/'She wears earrings.'

Talk through these differences and try to decide: a) what the
translators were trying to achieve; b) which you felt to be the most
successful attempt and why.

The various small groups could then report back their findings
and conclusions to the whole group.

See pages 94 – 5 for another example of this exercise.

# 13 KEY QUESTIONS II

**'The Bicycle Race'** *Michael Anthony*

At first sight this description might seem to be a straightforward account of a bicycle race, set on the island of Trinidad. But the closer you look at it, the more puzzling it becomes. Who is spectating? Who is competing? In what ways are they related?

## THE BICYCLE RACE

The afternoon sun blazed upon the games and the crowd had again and again roared itself hoarse, and now most of the events of the great day were accomplished. Towards the covered stands end the high-jump was going on and that caused a great bulge in the crowd on that side. Between the high-jump pit and the Commentator's Point was the rostrum, and as the events had come and gone, many had mounted the rostrum and had received prizes from the Prime Minister's wife, and smiled, and disappeared into the crowd again.

Now upon the green, on the inner track, many of the cyclists and athletes lay strewn, some exhausted, and most were in groups and talked together, and you could see by their gestures that they were explaining how the race went. The few who had not performed yet were limbering and warming up, and when they jogged round they stopped and shook hands and patted backs and they looked so jumpy you could tell how scared they were.

The father leaned against the railings and saw all this and he knew there was hardly anyone more scared than he. His moment was near now, it had come right up. It was already announced on the air. When the announcer had said, 'Competitors for the Fifteen Mile Blue Riband, please report to the Competitor's Steward,' he had felt a slight pain in his belly, as though he had wanted to go somewhere for a while. Now he put his left hand across the boy's shoulder, and the boy's perspiring fingers gripped his own. The cycle track was being cleared of straggler cyclists and the track stewards were warding off people who were easing too near the edge of the track. The cyclists had already gathered at the pavilion side, and the place had become very hushed and tense, and even the exhausted athletes on the

72

grass got up to watch. The father still felt the slight pain in his belly and there was a bad dryness in his mouth and he kept moistening his lips with his tongue. His heart was thumping against the back of the boy's head. He did not look towards the covered stand now, nor did he look down at the boy. He just gripped the boy's fingers tighter, and he felt as if drops of sweat were beginning to ooze through his hair.

The boy said nothing and he hardly moved. The pressure from behind had increased and he had already slipped right in front of his father so his father could take the weight. He saw that the vast field of cyclists were in order now and he heard the whistle signals of the race stewards, and he said to himself, 'Oh, God!' and he wanted to cross himself but he was ashamed. They saw the starter with the red jockey cap standing right behind the field of cyclists at the ready. All the other events were held up. The starter raised the pistol. The boy trembled distinctly and now he crossed himself.

The blast of the pistol swept off the Blue Riband riders and there were shouts and curses and skirmishes and spills, even before all the cyclists had cleared the starting line. The crowd broke into a roar again and everyone seemed calling on his favourite to break away. Many nonentities were leading in the first lap but no one took them seriously. There were screams for Hamille and Leon and George Willey, and already the Saddle Boys' supporters were making a deafening noise for Spence. But the race was not really warmed up yet and the stars were just getting the feel of the track. Leon was sitting well behind and all he was concerned with at the moment was to avoid being brought down. At the club-house he saw the leaders whizzing round in front of the pavilion, and now with the end of the first lap there were fifty-nine more laps to go. The end of this race would bring down the curtain on the First Day.

After twenty laps the field thinned out a good deal. Cecil Spence was now in front and George Willey and Sal Phillips were shadowing him. George Willey and Sal Philips were the two Siparia stars, and all the other cyclists had bunched right up to prevent those three getting away. Spence was riding cool, right on the inside of the track, his wheel grazing the line. Every time he passed in front of the uncovered stands the Saddle Boys' crowd drowned everything with 'Cecil! Cecil!' and there were supporters standing on the fringe of the track to hand him ice.

Leon had moved up near the head of the race. He was feeling comfortable now and controlled and here was where he'd stay for a little time. He wasn't going out in front today. He just wanted to be within hitting distance. He knew Spence was up to something, but he wasn't sure what. He was keeping his eyes on Spence and also on Sal and on George Willey. He held his handle-bar low, ready for anything. Yet he hoped he wouldn't be drawn out too early. He didn't think he'd go, unless things looked really bad.

The cyclists sped around and the pace was growing hot. Spence realized this and he was trying to keep in front and slow down the race, but he could see from the formation behind him that this would not work today. Some of the stars were restive but none of them wanted to go: they were watching Spence. They knew Spence's tactics and they didn't want the race slowed down. Spence guessed what was passing through their minds. He saw the crowding on the incline above him, and he kept his wheel on the line and ground the pedals a litle more.

He was a little worried because he was not riding his usual race. His usual race was from behind. He knew they had plans to heat up the race and he had gone out in front to try to control it. Everybody knew he was the man with the final burst, and as far as he was concerned, once he got a slow race he could beat anybody. Perhaps there was one man who would be tough. He reached out for ice and he tried to shake off that bitter memory of Siparia. Nevertheless he glanced through his arms. Then he looked to the outside to see who was there. Spence who had feared no man was today uneasy about just one. He gripped his handle-bar tight, and when he glanced through his arm it was only Knolly Prestor that had moved up behind him.

In the forty-first lap Ironman Hamille broke away. The crowd went haywire and even the Saddle Boys could not be heard. All round the ground there were cries of 'Ironman! Ironman!' and it was easy to tell he was on his home track. The field chased after him but two rounds later he was almost a quarter of a lap away. Prestor was going after him but the crowd shouted down Prestor because they wanted Hamille to get away.

Hamille was a Pointe-a-Pierre man and so was Prestor and the home crowd did not care much now so long as an outsider did not win. Prestor wanted to go but he was ashamed and held back. Hamille kept moving away from the field. Spence suddenly got off his saddle and his eyes were like a hawk's and he pumped, and he began streaking away like grease. Matthews got up too, and Alvin Levis, and the three of them were like arrows in the sun, but after a while it became clear that Hamille was holding them off and the crowd was in pandemonium and some of the men threw away their hats.

Leon looked across at Hamille. He got up from the saddle and he eased his way right up on the outside. If Hamille went any further away he'd have to go, whether the crowd shouted him down or not. It did not matter a damn that he was a Pointe-a-Pierre Club man. This was a race and they were all fighting to win. He was ready to cut down anybody, whatever the club. He did not train all these wretched months to look after Pointe-a-Pierre Club men. He went right up to the front and was ready to pounce.

As he watched Hamille go into the wind he saw his chest bobbing up and down which made it clear he was blowing through his mouth. No man riding like that at this stage could keep it up. Leon sat down again. Ah, Hamille, boy, he thought.

It was not until the fiftieth lap that the field caught up with Hamille, but the uproar did not subside. Prestor tried to break away but he could not hold it and it looked as though George Willey was biding his time. Leon was at George Willey's back wheel. The field was well strung out now and Hamille had so broken the lesser cyclists that now only fifteen out of the fifty-six starters remained. The excitement reached fever pitch.

At the front there was a group of eight and the rest did not seem to be seriously in the race. A big crowd of Pointe-a-Pierre Club supporters had gathered on the inner track and every time the group passed they cried, 'Leon!' 'Go Knolly!' and there were some Whizz Wheelers who cried, 'Matthews!' No one called upon Hamille now as Hamille was weakening. He had used up too much energy in his bid and now he wanted to catch a second wind. He wanted the pace slowed down but neither Preston nor Leon would do it, and he did not have enough in his legs to get out in front. In the fifty-fifth lap he rode into the inner track and gave up.

Leon was ready to swoop. Prestor and Alvin Levis were in front of him and when he looked between his arms he could see Matthews and there was the jersey of a Whizz Wheeler in his view. He did not know who the Whizz Wheeler was and he did not care. He thought of Prestor in front of him and he wondered how much Prestor had in him still. To him, Prestor was the only man who still looked strong. Prestor was his friend but really he had no friend, no, not in this game, and he told himself by Christ it would be blasted blood and sand after that bell. His front wheel was so close to Prestor's that they were almost rubbing. He was feeling good. He told himself he rode a damn good race so far. He told himself he did not ride such a damn fine race to come up here and lose. As they flew round at the pavilion side the board showed it was lap fifty-eight.

He looked through his arms now to see who was jostling for position. He was feeling strong and brutal. He was startled by the power in him for he had never been in such a hot race before and now even Spence had been killed off. Spence and the great Hamille. He looked at Alvin Levis grinding on the outside and he said to himself, Alvin boy, I didn't know you was so fiery!

The shouting was mad now and he heard the crowd calling on him, and the people on the edge of the track were wild with excitement, and there were those who wanted to give him ice. He did not want any ice. He moved into the wind now, taking the fifty-ninth lap and the group was bunching up closer, and every man was marking the other. He kept his wheel almost on to Prestor's but as he moved past the sight-screen, he heard the voice cry, 'Move out for Christ sake! Get on the outside!' and he heard the small voice shout, 'Lee-on!'

75

He felt as though aflame. The field was crowding badly and it was not so easy to move out. Prestor was either weakening or deliberately holding him back. The pace was getting blistering. He was desperate. He wanted to move out in time for the bell and he could not get out on the side and Prestor was not riding to let him out.

Coming for the bell Alvin Levis broke away and there was a scream from the crowd. Leon looked wildly about him. He called on Prestor for gangway but Prestor was burnt out and could not move. He saw that Matthews and the Whizz Wheeler, Ralph Hackett, were boxing him in and his head went hot. The bell clanged and dust drifted in front of the pavilion and as they swept past the covered stand he heard the shrill cry of a girl.

He had had to check and now he was last behind. Now he had a clearway on the outside. He had to make the Wasp fly now. He had to make the Wasp talk! He got off the saddle and hammered with everything he had in him.

Half a lap to go and Guaracara Park was a shouting, screaming din. Alvin Levis was half a bicycle ahead and Matthews was holding off Leon by half a wheel. Hackett the Whizz Wheeler slid back and there was nothing of Prestor at all. Leon set his teeth and ground and pounded and the blue Wasp began to sing. Matthews grimaced and hammered but Leon's front wheel gradually eased away from him. And now Leon was collaring Levis and the two bikes had drawn almost level. Pandemonium broke loose and the crowd jumped the railings to race towards the finish line. The Stewards fought and shouted to keep them edging in on the track. The two cyclists hammered, Alvin Levis holding his own, and the shouting shook the place. Now they took the home straight. Leon's head hung forward and he pushed and pounded until the tissues of his belly felt as though they would be ripped away. He was in the very last of his strength. His face twisted in agony, and his lips were skinned and were white with the dust, and he rocked and jerked the bike, and now his tyre found a little edge in front and as he struggled to maintain it chaos broke over the grounds. The little boy clung to his father. The father's face was drenched with sweat and he was jumping and shouting. 'Now!' he cried, 'Now! N-Now!' and as the dust kicked, and the flag went up, he was overwhelmed and he wept.

*Michael Anthony*

Have another look at the 'step by step' suggestions for tackling 'The Place' on page 40.

See if you can use them to make more sense of this story.

First read through this play script, an extract from *City Sugar.*

## CITY SUGAR

*(The setting is a studio of Leicester Sound, a local commercial radio station. Leonard Brazil is the disc-jockey, Rex is his engineer.)*

**Leonard:** *(swinging round to the mike and switching on the monitor speakers, fading down the end of the record)* And now, a special competition. You heard me – a mind-tingling competition. And by my side is the ever dependable Rex, sweating slightly, what have we got as a prize, Rex?

**Rex:** *(nervous, standing by the mike and speaking into it, putting on an almost BBC voice)* We have *their* latest LP – the Yellow Jack's latest!

**Leonard:** *(brash voice)* Tell us the title, Rex – *please* tell us the title.

**Rex:** 'High Up There.'

**Leonard:** That's a fine title – is it a fine record?

**Rex:** It's very exciting Leonard, it really is. . .

**Leonard:** *(to the listeners)* And you can have it a whole two or three weeks before it's in the shops, one of the very first in the whole country to have it. And what is Rex going to make us do?. . .Well, I think he's been fiddling with his tapes.

**Rex:** I have indeed –

**Leonard:** Very posh today aren't we, Rex?

**Rex:** Are we, Leonard?

**Leonard:** And what have you done with your tapes?

**Rex:** I've slowed them down – rather a lot.

**Leonard:** Slowed them down – we're getting even more posh.

**Rex:** Yes.

**Leonard:** *(loud)* Tell me Rex, what effect does this have on the listener?

**Rex:** What?

**Leonard:** *(very fast)* What effect does this have on the *listener?*
**Rex:** What. . .well it. . .(Rex *dries completely, stands helpless.*) I. . .

(Leonard *presses the button: a tape of the Leicester Sound jingle cuts off* Rex's *floundering.*)

**Leonard:** Enough of this gibberish. *(Normal voice.)* O.K. sweets – this is it. Rex is going to play one of the songs in the Top *Eleven,* and it has been slo-o-o-o-owed do-o-o-own, so it sounds a little different. And you're going to give us the singer and the song aren't you. . . Double five three zero four is the number to ring. . .that's right. *(Bogart voice.)* Play it again, Rex.

(Rex *back in his box, switches on a tape of 'The Proud One' by the Osmonds at 16 rpm.*)

**Leonard:** *(after a few bars, reducing the volume on the monitor speakers, he talks into the intercom to* Rex; *off the air)* Sounds a little more exciting like this doesn't it. I shall always play it like this in the future. *(Suddenly loud.)* All records will be played at *eight* rpm, and we'll talk that slowly too.

(Rex *has come out of the box.*)

**Rex:** I'm. . .sorry about messing things up, I didn't mean to. . .
**Leonard:** Of course you didn't –
**Rex:** You took me by surprise, I didn't think. . .I'm sorry, I won't do it again.
**Leonard:** No of course you won't. You won't get another chance to. Now get back into your box where you belong. *(He returns to the mike; switches it to go live again. Loud.)* Rex – what have you done to my favourite song? How's that for first-degree murder – a fine song slo-o-o-owly tortured to death. OK, sweets, who can be the first caller – race to your phones, dial furiously. . .I'm touching the first prize now – all fourteen tracks of it. . .we're handling the two of them with rubber gloves up here – and forceps, and we're keeping them in an incubator at night, in case we can hatch a third. Seriously now – *(He's put his headphones on.)* – we have a caller; and the first caller is. . .

**A girl's voice:** *(on the telephone, amplified through the monitors)* Hello? Hello. . .
**Leonard:** *(softly)* Hello there. . .what's your name, love?
**Girl:** Angela. . .
**Leonard:** Lovely. Have we ever talked before?
**Angela:** No, never –

**Leonard:** Fine. You at home Angela?

**Angela:** Yeah – I'm at home.

**Leonard:** Good – well, let's go straight into it Angela, into the un-known. . .*(Signalling to Rex, who switches on the slowed-down tape again, in the background.)* Who do you think the noise is, this *slo-o-ow* noise?

**Angela:** Is it – 'The Proud One' by the Osmonds?

**Leonard:** Did you say –

**Angela:** *(about to correct herself).* I. . .

**Leonard:** Angela, you're r-r-r-o-o-o-o-ight! Well done! (Rex *speeds up the record to the right speed, it plays a few bars.* Leonard *signals to* Rex *and the volume is reduced.)* There we go – clever girl. I'm dropping your prize into Rex's hand, to be wiped spotless, and posted, jet-propelled towards you Angela. Bye, love. Let's have the next one Rex *(A slowed-down version of 'I Can't Give You Anything (But My Love)' by the Stylistics.* Leonard *gets up again.)* This is an easy kill for them – they use their record-players so much at home, they all run slowly anyway. . .those who *have* record-players.

**Rex:** *(staring at* Leonard) I really like it, you know – *(Slight smile.)* – if I'm allowed to say so, how you always touch something when you're talking about it, even if it's the wrong record, like just now.

**Leonard:** Yes. I like that too. It's the actor in me. It's what makes it reasonably good. *(Staring round the studio.)* Where is the nauseating object anyway? *(Sees the Yellow Jacks LP, picks it up.)* Have you read the back, with Ross – *(American voice.)* – the lead singer speak-ing *his mind. (Normal voice.)* Take an example at random – and this is a nice lad from Bolton speaking – Ross numbers among his favourite things: walnut ice-cream, honeysuckle, genuine people, starfish, and sunburnt bare feet.' *(Loud.)* You realise we're going to have to play the utterances of this jellied imbecile all this week – the promoters have sent us a long tape, in a silk case, and the station's excited too, they want it to be a lively few days; I keep getting little illiterate messages from Johnson pushed under the door saying, 'Please remember, *maximum* required.' *(He switches on the mike sud-denly.)* Hello – what's your name please?

**Girl's voice:** Rita.

**Leonard:** *(slight smile)* Lovely Rita, Meter Maid?

**Rita:** What?

**Leonard:** A reference to years gone by, don't let it worry you, Rita. Have we talked before?

**Rita:** No.

**Leonard:** You listen often –

**Rita:** Yes. . .yes I do.

**Leonard:** *(smiles, soft)* Good, that's how it should be. Let's go straight into it then love, into the nitty gritty – who do you think it is?

**Rita:** I think it's – *(She gives the wrong title.)*

**Leonard:** Well, Rita, you're wrong, I'm afraid.

**Rita:** No I'm not. . .am I?

**Leonard:** I'm afraid so.

**Rita:** You sure?. . .*(Louder.)* I was certain. You –

**Leonard:** *(cutting her off)* I'm sorry love, you're wrong; keep listening though, for a very important reason. . .bye for now. *(Hughie Green voice.)* And let's go straight in to the next contestant! Coming up to Big John with the news at three o'clock. One down, one LP to go – round, crisp and shiny. What's your name please?

**Nicola's voice:** *(extremely flat, unemotional)* Hello.

**Leonard:** A little louder please – what's your name?

**Nicola:** *(very quiet)* Nicola Davies.

**Leonard:** A little louder.

**Nicola:** *(loud)* Nicola Davies.

**Leonard:** Nicola Davies. That's very formal. Are you at home, Nicola Davies?

**Nicola:** Yes.

**Leonard:** *(suddenly interested)* And what are you wearing, Nicola?

**Nicola:** Trousers. . .

**Leonard:** A little louder – you've got a very nice voice, Nicola. You're wearing trousers, and anything else?

**Nicola:** Yes. . .shoes.

**Leonard:** Shoes, that's an interesting picture, she's wearing just trousers and shoes. Only wish we had television phones, sexy Nicola . . .so, to win this LP, that Rex is just slipping into its beautiful see-through tight-fitting sleeve – who is it, Nicola?

**Nicola:** It's the Stylistics and – *(She gives the wrong title.)*

**Leonard:** I'm afraid, Nicola. . .

**Nicola:** *(correcting herself)* No, it's 'I Can't Give You Anything (But My Love).'

**Leonard:** Well Nicola – I'm afraid your first answer is the only one I can accept. . .

**Nicola:** Oh. . .

**Leonard:** But you were very close – and so, as you've given us *all* your name, Nicola Davies – I'm going, actually, to give it to you.

**Nicola:** Oh good – thank you.

**Leonard:** Just for you, Nicola Davies, but on one condition – and that is –

**Nicola:** *(Nervous)* What is that?

**Leonard:** You listen for just one more moment, because I have something rather extraordinary to announce to everyone. . .I'm going to be running many competitions this week for all ages – but one of them is different – for, to tie in with the great Yellow Jacks' concert here in this city on Saturday we're running 'The Competition of the Century'. . .and the prize is actually meeting one of the boys. How do you like that, Nicola Davies?

**Nicola:** Yes. . .what do you do?

**Leonard:** And not only that – the winner will ride to London, after the concert, in *their* car, sitting with *them,* and what is more they will then spend four days in London, the capital of this fine country, at the expense of Leicester Sound. That's OK, isn't it? – Nicola?

**Nicola:** Yes. . .what do –

**Leonard:** *(cutting her off)* So everybody tune in tomorrow, for the first stage – you too Nicola – *(His voice quieter, smiles.)* – you never know – what your luck might be – we might even speak again. *(He puts down the phone. Drops his biro onto the desk. Pause. Quiet.)*
We're off.

*(Blackout)*

*Stephen Poliakoff*

As well as giving scope for activities such as the 'improvised conversations' (see page 44) [you could try being Leonard Brazil], or 'answering in role' (see page 57), [let Rex and Nicola put Leonard on the spot for once!], this extract also gives you an opportunity to record a whole scene on tape.

Firstly you will need to work it through in small groups several times.

There are also some questions you will need to answer as a group:

— Why does Leonard talk like that?

— What is he up to?

— What sort of effect does he have on the others, especially Rex and Nicola?

You will also have to decide on the sound effects you intend to use.

If this works well, you might like to go on to predict a suitable 'Competition of the Century' for Leicester Sound. What might Nicola's role in it be?

# 15 FINDING YOUR OWN WAY INTO A STORY

'The Use of Force' *William Carlos Williams*

Almost any of the approaches suggested so far could be successfully used with this story 'The Use of Force'. However, there comes a time when you need to stand on your own two feet and find your own way into a story or poem. See what you can make of it.

## THE USE OF FORCE

They were new patients to me, and all I had was the name, Olson. Please come down as soon as you can, my daughter is very sick.

When I arrived I was met by the mother, a big startled looking woman, very clean and apologetic who merely said, Is this the doctor? and let me in. In the back she added, You must excuse us, doctor, we have her in the kitchen where it is warm. It is very damp here sometimes.

The child was fully dressed and sitting on her father's lap near the kitchen table. He tried to get up, but I motioned for him not to bother, took off my overcoat and started to look things over. I could see that they were all very nervous, eyeing me up and down distrustfully. As often, in such cases, they weren't telling me more than they had to, it was up to me to tell them; that's why they were spending three dollars on me.

The child was fairly eating me up with her cold, steady eyes, and no expression to her face whatever. She did not move and seemed, inwardly, quiet; an unusually attractive little thing, and as strong as a heifer in appearance. But her face was flushed, she was breathing rapidly, and I realized that she had a high fever. She had magnificent blonde hair, in profusion. One of those picture children often reproduced in advertising leaflets and the photogravure sections of the Sunday papers.

She's had a fever for three days, began the father and we don't know what it comes from. My wife has given her things, you know, like people do, but it don't do no good. And there's been a lot of sickness around. So we tho't you'd better look her over and tell us what is the matter.

As doctors often do I took a trial shot at it as a point of departure. Has she had a sore throat?

Both parents answered me together, No. . .No, she says her throat don't hurt her.

Does your throat hurt you? added the mother to the child. But the little girl's expression didn't change nor did she move her eyes from my face.

Have you looked?

I tried to, said the mother, but I couldn't see.

As it happens we had been having a number of cases of diphtheria in the school to which this child went during that month and we were all, quite apparently, thinking of that, though no one had as yet spoken of the thing.

Well, I said, suppose we take a look at the throat first. I smiled in my best professional manner and asking for the child's first name I said, come on, Mathilda, open your mouth and let's take a look at your throat.

Nothing doing.

Aw, come on, I coaxed, just open your mouth wide and let me take a look. Look, I said opening both hands wide, I haven't anything in my hands. Just open up and let me see.

Such a nice man, put in the mother. Look how kind he is to you. Come on, do what he tells you to. He won't hurt you.

At that I ground my teeth in disgust. If only they wouldn't use the word 'hurt' I might be able to get somewhere. But I did not allow myself to be hurried or disturbed but speaking quietly and slowly I approached the child again.

As I moved my chair a little nearer suddenly with one cat-like movement both her hands clawed instinctively for my eyes and she almost reached them too. In fact she knocked my glasses flying and they fell, though unbroken, several feet away from me on the kitchen floor.

Both the mother and father almost turned themselves inside out in embarrassment and apology. You bad girl, said the mother, taking her and shaking her by one arm. Look what you've done. The nice man...

For heaven's sake, I broke in. Don't call me a nice man to her. I'm here to look at her throat on the chance that she might have diphtheria and possibly die of it. But that's nothing to her. Look here, I said to the child, we're going to look at your throat. You're old enough to understand what I'm saying. Will you open it now by yourself or shall we have to open it for you?

Not a move. Even her expression hadn't changed. Her breaths however were coming faster and faster. Then the battle began. I had to do it. I had to have a throat culture for her own protection. But first I told the parents that it was entirely up to them. I explained the danger but said that I would not insist on a throat examination so long as they would take the responsibility.

If you don't do what the doctor says you'll have to go to the hospital, the mother admonished her severely.

Oh yeah? I had to smile to myself. After all, I had already fallen in love with the savage brat, the parents were contemptible to me. In the ensuing struggle they grew more and more abject, crushed, exhausted while she surely rose to magnificent heights of insane fury of effort bred of her terror of me.

The father tried his best, and he was a big man but the fact that she was his daughter, his shame at her behavior and his dread of hurting her made him release her just at the critical moment several times when I had almost achieved success, till I wanted to kill him. But his dread also that she might have diphtheria made him tell me to go on, go on though he himself was almost fainting, while the mother moved back and forth behind us raising and lowering her hands in agony of apprehension.

Put her in front of you on your lap, I ordered, and hold both her wrists.

But as soon as he did the child let out a scream. Don't, you're hurting me. Let go of my hands. Let them go I tell you. Then she shrieked terrifyingly, hysterically. Stop it! Stop it! You're killing me!

Do you think she can stand it, doctor! said the mother.

You get out, said the husband to his wife. Do you want her to die of diphtheria?

Come on now, hold her, I said.

Then I grasped the child's head with my left hand and tried to get the wooden tongue depressor between her teeth. She fought, with clenched teeth, desperately! But now I also had grown furious – at a child. I tried to hold myself down but I couldn't. I know how to expose a throat for inspection. And I did my best. When finally I got the wooden spatula behind the last teeth and just the point of it into the mouth cavity, she opened up for an instant but before I could see anything she came down again and gripping the wooden blade between her molars she reduced it to splinters before I could get it out again.

Aren't you ashamed, the mother yelled at her. Aren't you ashamed to act like that in front of the doctor?

Get me a smooth-handled spoon of some sort, I told the mother. We're going through with this. The child's mouth was already bleeding. Her tongue was cut and she was screaming in wild hysterical shrieks. Perhaps I should have desisted and come back in an hour or more. No doubt it would have been better. But I have seen at least two children lying dead in bed of neglect in such cases, and feeling guilty that I must get a diagnosis now or never I went at it again. But the worst of it was that I too had got beyond reason. I could have torn the child apart in my own fury and enjoyed it. It was a pleasure to attack her. My face was burning with it.

The damned little brat must be protected against her own idiocy, one says to one's self at such times. Others must be protected against her. It is a social necessity. And all these things are true. But a blind fury, a feeling of adult shame, bred of a longing for muscular release are the operatives. One goes on to the end.

In a final unreasoning assault I overpowered the child's neck and jaws. I forced the heavy silver spoon back of her teeth and down her throat till she gagged. And there it was — both tonsils covered with membrane. She had fought valiantly from knowing her secret. She had been hiding that sore throat for three days at least and lying to her parents in order to escape just such an outcome as this.

Now truly she *was* furious. She had been on the defensive before but now she attacked. Tried to get off her father's lap and fly at me while tears of defeat blinded her eyes.

*William Carlos Williams*

After discussing the story for a while a group of fifteen-year-olds came up with these two suggestions:

1   Try retelling the story entirely through the eyes of the child.
2   Listen in to the *conversations off the page* — what might have been happening in the Olson household before and after the Doctor's visit?

They follow. What would be your way in to the story?

### The use of force
### (a) through the child's view:

Doctors are new to me, my throat hurts, and I find it hard to speak, but I don't want to see any doctor however nice Mum says he is. She said his name was Sinclair.

When he arrived, he was met by Mum. I was in the kitchen sitting on Dad's knee. Then for the first time I saw the man, I glared at him. I wasn't going to let him know. I studied every possible feature of the doctor. He had a beard which I think is very unhealthy, he was quite tall, had dark brown hair and very bushy eyebrows, which I didn't like. My Dad tried to get up but the doctor waved his hand and Dad sat down again. He just stood in the doorway for the first few minutes without doing anything, just looking at me with a dazed look. I glared back. Then he asked if I'd had a sore throat, stupid man. I wasn't going to tell him anything. I just kept on staring. I knew it was bad manners but I didn't like him. Then he said that he'd better have a look at my throat. The cheek of it. I wasn't going to let him. No way. Then he asked my name. I hated my name, Mum told him, then he approached me saying, 'Come on Mathilda, open your mouth.' That did it, I reached for him and tried to scratch him. I hit his glasses onto the floor and felt quite pleased with myself until my Mum shouted at me and shook me by the arm.

The doctor then tried a different tactic. By treating me like a grown up hoping that I'd co-operate like an adult would, but I wasn't falling for that trick. Then he had the audacity to threaten me saying he would make me open my mouth. But I was finding it harder to breathe. He said something to my parents about danger and my Mum said I'd have to go to hospital if I didn't let the doctor look at my throat. I hated him, hated, hated...My Dad took hold of me. I kicked and screamed, I wanted to hurt him. I hated him. My Mum wasn't helping much, she was just pacing up and down. Then she grabbed me and put me over her lap and held my wrists. I screamed stop, you're hurting me, let go, stop it, stop it, you're killing me. It was having its effect on Mum, but not the doctor. Then something was thrust in my mouth, I bit it, pain shot through my mouth. My Mum yelled at me, the doctor's beard was turning grey at the edges (or so I thought) and he was red in the face. Then Mum gave him a metal spoon, he thrust it towards my mouth, my mouth yielded with the pressure he'd exerted and the spoon opened my mouth. His bushy eyebrows and beard loomed closer. Then I struggled as he learnt my secret and tears blurred my vision.

### (b) overheard conversations between Mr and Mrs Olson and Mathilda:

**BEFORE THE DOCTOR'S VISIT:**

*Scene: A small kitchen warmed by a small fire, in the middle a large wooden table with six chairs round it. In the corner sits a man about 40 and on his knee a thin child is perched; she is close to tears. A large woman is standing up near the door waiting.*

**Mrs Olson:** Do you think we've done the right thing you know how much these people cost. She can't be that ill or she would have told us, wouldn't you, Mathilda?
(*Mr Olson gave Mathilda a sharp nudge which aroused her from her thought. For a moment, she was unable to reply, but after a moment she gave a small feeble cough and began to speak in a husky way.*)
**Mathilda:** Yes Mum, you know me. I tell everyone!
**Mr Olson:** I think it's bad, why must she hide things from us. It was the same when she had to go to hospital for that operation. She never said anything about the pain, until that night when it got real bad. Why do it, Mat?

*(Mathilda cringed at the thought of her last incident with a doctor. She resented doctors, she always had. They made her do things she didn't want. Mathilda was unable to tell anyone of her troubles, she was going to hide her illness. It would go away soon, wouldn't it? She looked up to her father and smiled.)*

**Mr Olson:** You're always so happy, how do you manage to be so weak but always have a smile. Why is it we all are ill so often?

**Mrs Olson:** I blame this house, it's as damp as anything during the winter, but as we can't afford much else, it will have to do. Life's hard to those who can't afford it, isn't it?

*(Mathilda nodded and returned to her own thoughts: I wonder what really is wrong with me, if only this sore throat would go away, and the growths on my tonsils. What can it be? If only the doctor wasn't coming.)*
*(There was a knock on the door.)*
*(Oh, no, thought Mathilda, he's here. Her whole body froze, unable to do anything.)*

**AFTER THE DOCTOR'S VISIT:**

*Scene: The small kitchen looked like a junk yard, chairs everywhere. In the corner where Mr Olson had sat was Mathilda, sprawled on the floor crying her eyes out. Mrs and Mrs Olson were stood in the corner talking. The doctor had left to phone for an ambulance to take Mathilda to hospital.*

**Mrs Olson:** Why is it always her who gets these things? Diphtheria is a killer, isn't it? Why our Mat? Poor little mite. Doctor said it wasn't in the serious stage yet, so there's hope where there's life.

**Mr Olson:** Calm down dear, you're hysterical. He'll do his best for her.

*(Mathilda was still crying, her whole life seemed to be flashing by her at tremendous speed. She sank onto her knees and watched the world move. Her life was coming to an abrupt ending, she thought. Why had she not told anyone before? Why keep this, of all things, a secret? Life to her was awful, she wanted to die now, not live after she had put her parents through this. It was cruel. But then she suddenly changed her mind. Say he got this wrong, it could be just a sore throat. That's it, a bad throat. No, she kicked herself, doctors round here are always right! Shortly after this he returned, the doctor and his case. He walked over to Mathilda, gave her a sharp but pleasant look and told her parents to pack a bag and he would put Mat in the ambulance. She went with no struggle. Her life was going to be saved.)*

87

## 16 FINAL THOUGHTS: WORDS AND PICTURES

**'Market Economy'** *Marge Piercy*
**'Legs'** *Renta Snap*

We have chosen to place this poem next to this photograph.

Were we right to do this?

Does the presence of one help you to make more sense of the other? And what kind of sense is being made anyway? What do you think?

### THE MARKET ECONOMY

Suppose some peddlar offered
you can have a color TV
but your baby will be
born with a crooked spine;
you can have polyvinyl cups
and wash and wear
suits but it will cost
you your left lung
rotted with cancer; suppose
somebody offered you
a frozen precooked dinner
every night for ten years
but at the end
your colon dies
and then you do,
slowly and with much pain.
You get a house in the suburbs
but you work in a new plastics
factory and die at fifty-two
when your kidneys turn off.

But where else will you
work? where else can
you rent but Smog City?
The only houses for sale
are under the yellow sky.
You've been out of work for
a year and they're hiring
at the plastics factory.
Don't read the fine
print, there isn't any.

*Marge Piercy*

# MORE STORIES AND POEMS

## Stories

'The Table is a Table', Peter Bichsel from *Story One* ed. Jackson and Pepper (Penguin)

'Message from the Pig-Man', John Wain from *A John Wain Selection* (Longman)

'The Zoo', William Carlos Williams from *The Farmer's Daughters* (New Directions paperback)

'New York to Detroit', Dorothy Parker from *The Penguin Dorothy Parker* (Penguin)

'The Little Pet', Dan Jacobson from *A Way of Life* (Longman) or *Through the Wilderness* (Penguin)

'Beggar My Neighbour', Dan Jacobson from *A Way of Life* (Longman)

'You Should Have Seen The Mess', Muriel Spark from *Story 2* (Penguin)

'It Must be Different', Morley Callaghan from *Story 3* (Penguin)

'Jane is a Girl', Walter Macken from *The Coll Doll and Other Stories* (Macmillan)

'Manhood', John Wain from *Story 2* (Penguin)

'Sunday', Ted Hughes from *Wodwo* (Faber)

'The Rain Horse', Ted Hughes from *Modern short stories* ed. J. Hunter (Faber)

'Free Dinners', Farrukh Dhondy from *Come to Mecca* (Fontana Lion)

'Ant Lion', Judith Wright from *The Green Storyhouse* (Oxford University Press)

'The Fury', Stan Barstow from *The Human Element* (Longman)

'A Casual Acquaintance', Stan Barstow from *A Casual Acquaintance* (Longman)

'Gussy and the Boss', Samuel Selvon fom *Ways of Sunlight* (Longman)

'Coco', Larry Coles from *Openings* English Project (Ward Lock Educational)

'Stone Boy', Gina Berriault from *Bonds* English Project (Ward Lock Educational)

'Flight', Doris Lessing from *Story 3* (Penguin)

'In the Park', Judith Wright from *People Like Us* (Faber)

'Samuel', Grace Paley from *Enormous Changes at the Last Minute* (Virago)

'The Stone Thrower', Douglas Dunn from *The Story Inside* (Hutchinson)

## Poems

'15 Million Plastic Bags', Adrian Mitchell from *For Beauty Douglas* (Allison & Busby)

'History Lesson', Miroslav Holub from *Openings* English Project, (Ward Lock Educational)

'The Companion', Yevtushenko from *Selected Poems* (Penguin)

'Other Versions 1-3', D.J. Enright from *Rhyme Times Rhyme* (Chatto and Windus)

'First Blood', Jon Stallworthy from *Voices 2* (Penguin)

'Breakfast', Jacques Prévert from *Conflict 2* (Nelson)

'Child on top of a Greenhouse', Theodore Roethke from *Junior Voices 3* (Penguin)

'Questions from a Worker who Reads', Bertolt Brecht from *Worlds Apart* (Ward Lock Educational)

'Inspection', Wilfred Owen from *War Poems and Others* (Chatto and Windus)

'The Explosion', Philip Larkin from *High Windows* (Faber)

'Unknown Citizen', W.H. Auden from *W.H. Auden : A Selection* (Hutchinson)

'Leaflets', Adrian Mitchell from *Worlds* ed. Geoffrey Summerfield (Penguin)

'We're Going to see the Rabbit', Alan Brownjohn from *7 Themes in Modern Verse* (Harrap)

'Legend', Judith Wright from *Ventures* (Ward Lock Educational)

'A Brown Paper Carrierbag', Roger McGough from *Poems 2* (Oxford University Press)

'Good Taste', Christopher Logue from *Poems 2* (Oxford University Press)

'At the Bomb Testing Site', William Stafford from *The Rattle Bag* (Faber)

'The Vacuum', Howard Nemerov from *Family and School* English Project (Ward Lock Educational)

'Blackberry Picking', Seamus Heaney *Voices 2* (Penguin)

# APPENDIX 1

The complete version of:

## THE SECRET IN THE CAT

I took my cat apart
to see what made him purr.
Like an electric clock
or like the snore

of a warming kettle,
something fizzled and sizzled in him.
Was he a soft car,
the engine bubbling sound?

Was there a wire beneath his fur,
or humming throttle?
I undid his throat.
Within was no stir.

I opened up his chest
as though it were a door:
no whisk or rattle there.
I lifted off his skull:

no hiss or murmur.
I halved his little belly
but found no gear,
no cause for static.

So I replaced his lid,
laced his little gut.
His heart into his vest I slid
and buttoned up his throat.

His tail rose to a rod
and beckoned to the air.
Some voltage made him vibrate
warmer than before.

Whiskers and a tail:
perhaps they caught
some radar code
emitted as a pip, a dot-and-dash

of woollen sound.
My cat a kind of tuning fork? –
amplifier? – telegraph? –
doing secret signal work?

His eyes elliptic tubes:
there's a message in his stare.
I stroke him
but cannot find the dial.

*May Swenson*

# APPENDIX 2

Another 'alternative version' as well as an interesting beginning:
'The Singer' from *The Caucasian Chalk Circle* by Bertolt Brecht.

## THE SINGER

In olden times, in a bloody time,
There ruled in a Caucasian city –
Men called it City of the Damned –
A Governor.
His name was Georgi Abashwili.
He was rich as Croesus
He had a beautiful wife
He had a healthy baby.
No other governor in Grusinia
Had so many horses in his stable
So many beggars on his doorstep
So many soldiers in his service
So many petitioners in his courtyard.
Georgi Abashwili – how shall I describe him to you?
He enjoyed his life.
On the morning of Easter Sunday
The Governor and his family went to church.

*translated by Eric Bently*

**THE SINGER**

Once upon a time
A time of bloodshed
When this city was called
The city of the damned
It had a Governor.
His name was Georgi Abashvili
Once upon a time.

He was very rich
He had a beautiful wife
He had a healthy child
Once upon a time.

No other governor in Grusinia
Had as many horses in his stable
As many beggars on his doorstep
As many soldiers in his service
As many petitioners in his courtyard
Once upon a time.

Georgi Abashvili, how shall I describe him?
He enjoyed his life:
On Easter Sunday morning
The Governor and his family went to church
Once upon a time.

*translated by James Stern*
*and W.H. Auden*